KU-628-608

®

Japanese
in 30 Days

By Kazuko Imaeda

Berlitz Publishing
New York   Munich   Singapore

Copyright © 2007 by Apa Publications/Berlitz Publishing. Originally published by Cheng & Tsui Company, Inc., Boston, MA., U.S.A. This abridged edition published by arrangement with Cheng & Tsui Company. All rights reserved by Cheng & Tsui Company, Inc.

NO part of this book may be reproduced, stored in a retrieval system or transmitted in any form or means electronic, mechanical, photocopying, recording or otherwise, without prior written permission from Apa Publications.

Contacting the Editors
Every effort has been made to provide accurate information in this publication, but changes are inevitable. The publisher cannot be responsible for any resulting loss, inconvenience or injury. We would appreciate it if readers would call our attention to any errors or outdated information by contacting Berlitz Publishing, 193 Morris Avenue, Springfield, NJ 07081, USA. Fax: 1-908-206-1103. email: comments@berlitzbooks.com

Berlitz Trademark Reg. U.S. Patent Office and other countries. Marca Registrada. Used under license from Berlitz Investment Corporation

Cover photo © Jupiter Images; inset photo © PhotoAlto

Publishing Director: Sheryl Olinsky Borg
Editor/Project Manager: Emily Bernath
Senior Editor: Lorraine Sova
Editor: Monica Bentley

Printed in Hong Kong
First printing, Fall 2006

Contents

Introduction

Grammar: Japanese syllables ▪ how to read a Japanese word ▪ long vowels ▪ double consonants

Grammar: tadaima ▪ meeting and greeting
Country & Culture: bowing

Grammar: singular and plural ▪ particles ▪ requests: **kudasai** ▪ the particles **to** and **ka**
Country & Culture: **irasshaimase**

Grammar: basic conversations ▪ linking verbs: *is, am, are* ▪ personal pronouns ▪ **-jin, -tachi**: describing yourself and others ▪ suffixes ▪ this, that and (that) over there for people: **kore, sore** and **are** ▪ talking abut family ▪ this that and (that) over there for places: **koko**, **soko** and **asoko**
Country & Culture: sitting; *Writing Exercise:* **a, i, u, e, o (hiragana)**

Grammar: asking questions ▪ yes and no: **hai** and **iie** ▪ negative statements ▪ interrogative pronouns
Country & Culture: **hai** ▪ personal seals; *Writing Exercise:* **ka, ki, ku, ke, ko (hiragana)**

Let's Pronounce Japanese!

Japanese Syllables

Japanese sentences are written with a combination of characters called **kanji**, **hiragana** and **katakana**. **Kanji** consists of old Chinese characters, and each **kanji** symbol represents a full word, phrase or idea. **Hiragana** and **katakana** are two "alphabets". Each character represents a syllable without any individual meaning, just like English letters. **Hiragana** is used to write Japanese, **Katakana** is used for foreign words that are now part of the Japanese vocabulary.

Because you are not yet able to read any of these characters, this book uses **rōmaji**; a way to write Japanese using the English alphabet.

Using **rōmaji**, the chart below shows all of the syllables included in **hiragana** and **katakana**. Each syllable is equivalent to one **hiragana** or **katakana** symbol. Study the chart below and listen to the CD until you are familiar with the syllables and their pronunciation.

	First third					Second third			
a	i	u	e	o	ga	gi	gu	ge	go
ka	ki	ku	ke	ko	za	ji	zu	ze	zo
sa	shi	su	se	so	da			de	do
ta	chi	tsu	te	to	ba	bi	bu	be	bo
na	ni	nu	ne	no	pa	pi	pu	pe	po
ha	hi	fu	he	ho					
ma	mi	mu	me	mo					
ya		yu		yo					
ra	ri	ru	re	ro					
wa				wo					
n									

3

All About Food

Dialogue 1

Waitress:	Irasshaimase.
Tom:	Konnichiwa. Tenpura o kudasai.
Waitress:	Hai.

***

Waitress:	Dōzo.
Tom:	Arigatō.

May I have Tempura Please?

Tom, an American, has just moved to Japan with his family. This is his first visit to a Japanese restaurant.

Waitress:	Hello and welcome!
Tom:	Good afternoon. May I have tempura please?
Waitress:	Certainly (Yes).

The waitress comes back with a dish of tempura.

Waitress:	Please.
Tom:	Thank you (for bringing the food).

Singular and Plural

Japanese nouns have no special forms to show whether they are singular or plural, and there are no articles (the, a, an) in Japanese. **Ringo** means *an apple, apples, some apples, the apple* or *the apples*. Similarly, most Japanese pronouns have no special forms to show whether they are singular or plural. Hence *this* and *these* have the same word, **kore**, in Japanese. Japanese verbs do not have different forms to indicate whether their subjects are singular or plural or whether they are first person, second person or third person. *Am, is* and *are* all have the same verb, **desu**, in Japanese.

Particles

Consider the English sentence *The cat chases the mouse*. The action word, or verb, is *chases*. The subject is the person or thing doing the chasing: *the cat*. What is being chased is the direct object: *the mouse*. The meaning of the sentence is very different if the cat and the mouse are interchanged, that is: *the mouse chases the cat.*

Japanese has little words called particles, usually made out of one or two syllables (such as **wa**, **ga** and **o**). Particles, not word order, indicate subjects and objects in sentences. For example, **o** is placed after direct objects and **wa / ga** is placed after subjects.

Regardless of word order, it is always clear in a Japanese sentence which word is the subject and which word is the direct object. Only verbs have fixed locations: the verb comes at the end of the sentence or just before if **ka / ne / yo** follows the verb. Japanese prepositions and conjunctions are also considered particles.

Requests: *Kudasai*

The simplest way to ask for something is to use the sentence structure: direct object + **o kudasai**.
Kudasai is the verb meaning *May I have ___ please?*
O is the particle that indicates that the preceeding word is the direct object.

May I have an apple please?	**Ringo o kudasai.**
May I have an orange please?	**Orenji o kudasai.**

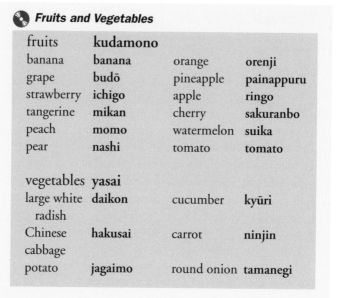

Fruits and Vegetables

fruits	kudamono		
banana	banana	orange	orenji
grape	budō	pineapple	painappuru
strawberry	ichigo	apple	ringo
tangerine	mikan	cherry	sakuranbo
peach	momo	watermelon	suika
pear	nashi	tomato	tomato

vegetables	yasai		
large white radish	daikon	cucumber	kyūri
Chinese cabbage	hakusai	carrot	ninjin
potato	jagaimo	round onion	tamanegi

Exercise 1

Listen to the food items, and match each with its English translation.

1. ___   **a.** sandwich
2. ___   **b.** watermelon
3. ___   **c.** apple
4. ___   **d.** coffee
5. ___   **e.** bread
6. ___   **f.** tangerine
7. ___   **g.** potato
8. ___   **h.** steak

The Particles To and Ka

The particle **to**, when used between nouns, is translated as
and or *both __ and __*.

an apple and a tangerine	***ringo to mikan***
a banana and a tangerine	***banana to mikan***
May I have both an apple and a tangerine please?	***Ringo to mikan o kudasai.***

The particle **ka**, when used between nouns, acts like the
English *or* or *either __ or __*.

an apple or an orange	***ringo ka orenji***
vegetables or fruits	***yasai ka kudamono***
May I have either an apple or an orange please?	***Ringo ka orenji o kudasai.***

 Let's Go to a Restaurant

In front of most restaurants in Japan, you will find a
window display showing various dishes. The names for
the dishes and their prices are displayed beside them.
The displays are helpful, but it's best to know what's
actually in the dishes. See the list below for some
typical Japanese menu items.

bowl of cooked rice with toppings of meat, fish, eggs and vegetables	**donburi**
hamburger	**hanbāgā**

juice	**jūsu**
Indian curry	**karēraisu**
coffee	**kōhī**
meat and vegetable pancake	**okonomiyaki**
bread	**pan**
ramen (hot soup with noodles)	**rāmen**
sandwich	**sandoicchi**
salad	**sarada**
buckwheat noodles eaten either with a cold dipping sauce or in a hot broth	**soba**
meat and vegetables cooked in sweetened soy sauce	**sukiyaki**
raw fish placed on top of vinegared rice balls or rolled with vinegared rice	**sushi**
steak	**sutēki**
tempura (pieces of food coated with thin batter and then deep fried)	**tenpura**
pork cutlet	**tonkatsu**
thick noodles in hot soup, garnished with meat and vegetables	**udon**
fried noodles with meat and vegetables (Chinese chow mein)	**yakisoba**
small chicken pieces skewered and barbequed with sauce	**yakitori**

Translate into English:

1. Banana o kudasai._____

2. Sushi o kudasai. _____

3. Sutēki to pan _____

4. Sutēki to pan o kudasai. _____

_____

5. Kōhī ka jūsū _____

6. Kōhī ka jūsū o kudasai. _____

_____

7. Ringo to mikan to banana o kudasai. _____

_____

Translate into rōmaji:

8. May I have apples please?_____

9. May I have Indian curry please? _____

10. A banana or an orange _____

11. May I have a banana or an orange please?_____

_____

12. Tempura and soba_____

13. May I have tempura and soba please? _____

_____

14. May I have coffee, bread and a pork cutlet please? _____

_____

Exercise 3

You are in a restaurant. Ask a waiter for the following dishes, using the sentence structure _ *o kudasai*. Say each sentence aloud, and check your answers on the CD.

1. hamburger   **2.** juice   **3.** salad
4. steak   **5.** coffee and sandwich

Irasshaimase

As soon as you step into a restaurant, you will hear *irasshaimase* from the waiters. Sometimes *irasshaimase* is said gently with a deep bow by the waiter in charge; more often, however, it is said loudly by many of them, one after another, from all quarters. *Irasshaimase* is a greeting to a customer when he or she comes into a restaurant or a shop. It is translated as *Hello and welcome!* or *Come in!*

You usually don't reply to these greetings unless you are friendly with the waiters or the shop clerks. You may also be greeted with *irasshaimase* when you visit someone's home.

Introduce Yourself

Dialogue 1

Tom:	Konnichiwa (Makoto-kun).
Makoto:	Konnichiwa (Tom-kun).
	Kore wa Sachiko desu.
	(Kore wa) imōto desu.
Sachiko:	Hajimemashite.
	Dōzo yoroshiku.
Tom:	Hajimemashite.
	(Boku wa) Tom desu.
	Dōzo yoroshiku.

How Do You Do?

Tom meets Makoto who is walking with his sister Sachiko.

Tom:	Good afternoon, Makoto.
Makoto:	Good afternoon, Tom.
	This is Sachiko.
	This is (my) younger sister.
Sachiko:	How do you do?
	Pleased to meet you.
Tom:	How do you do?
	I am Tom.
	Pleased to meet you.

A Few Words about Basic Conversations

When Japanese people speak, they omit parts of sentences that may be understood from the context or situation. To help you understand the conversations clearly in this book, such parts are included in parentheses. While practicing the conversations, omit the parts in parentheses. Note that, when a word is omitted from a conversation, the particle defining the purpose of the word in the sentence is omitted with it. For example, if a subject is omitted from a sentence, the particle **wa** is omitted also, as you see in the dialogue on page 17.

Linking Verbs: Is, Am, Are

To link subjects with complements in Japanese, use the intransitive verb **desu***.

<u>subject</u>   **wa**   <u>complement</u>   **desu**

The particle **wa** follows a subject, and the complement is placed before the intransitive verb **desu**, which comes at the end of the sentence.

Because Japanese verbs have no special forms to show whether their subjects are singular or plural, or whether they are of the first, second or third person, **desu** is translated as *is, am* or *are*.

*Although **desu** is defined as an auxiliary verb in Japanese grammar, we define it here as a linking verb since its main function is to equate one thing with another, like the English linking verb *to be*.

Personal Pronouns

Here are some important personal pronouns.

 I, me (for boys)   ***boku***
I, me (except boys)   ***watashi***
you   ***anata***

You may notice that boys use ***boku*** while everybody else uses ***watashi*** for *I* or *me*.

To introduce yourself, just use ***watashi*** (or ***boku***) for the subject and your name for the complement, in the sentence structure _ ***wa*** _ ***desu***.

 I am Tom.   ***Watashi wa Tom desu.***
I am Tom.   ***Boku wa Tom desu.***

-jin, -tachi: Describing Yourself and Others

Jin is a suffix added to the name of a country to stand for its person/people. Although Japanese nouns have the same form for singular and plural (both *an apple* and *apples* are ***ringo*** in Japanese), an exception applies to people. For people, we put ***tachi*** after nouns and personal pronouns to make them into the plural form. Hence ***watashi-tachi*** means *we* and ***Amerika-jin-tachi*** means *American people*.

By putting the following nouns in place of the complement, you may talk more about yourself.

 American person   **Amerika-jin**
German person   **Doitsu-jin**   ▶

19

French person	**Furansu-jin**
British person	**Igirisu-jin**
Canadian person	**Kanada-jin**
Japanese person	**Nihon-jin**
foreigner	**gaijin**
baby	**akachan**
child	**kodomo**
adult	**otona**
friend	**tomodachi**
student (of a school)	**gakusei**
dentist	**ha-isha**
physician, medical doctor	**isha**
white-collar worker	**kaishain**
nurse	**kangofu**
student (in general)	**seito**
teacher	**sensei**
waiter	**uētā**
waitress	**uētoresu**
I am an American.	**Watashi wa Amerika-jin desu.**
I am a student.	**Watashi wa gakusei desu.**

Suffixes

A Japanese person has two names, a family name and a given first name, and uses them in that order (for example, Hepburn Audrey). You may address a person by her family name or first given name, according to your degree of acquaintance, but the following suffix must be added to either name.

-chan   is added after the names of small children and especially after the names of girls; e.g., **Amy-chan**, *Amy.*

-kun   is added after the names of boys; e.g., **Bob-kun**, *Bob.*

-san   is added after names; it is comparable to Mr. or Ms.; e.g., **Smith-san**, *Mr./Ms. Smith;* **Betty-san**, *(Ms.) Betty.*

-sensei is added after the names of teachers (of any kind) and medical doctors; e.g., **Kelly-sensei**, *Mr./Ms./ Dr. Kelly.*

Suffixes should never be used when you are speaking about yourself. Teachers and medical doctors have a high social status in Japan, and, in the culture where showing respect for one another is important, it would be rude not to add **sensei** after their names.

You are Mr. Tom Kelly.   **Anata wa Kelly Tom-san desu.**
You are Makoto.   **Anata wa Makoto-kun desu.**
Hanako is a baby.   **Hanako-chan wa akachan desu.**

Exercise 1

🔊 Someone is introducing herself/himself to you. Listen carefully and answer the following questions in rōmaji by filling in the blanks.

1. Who am I?

Anata wa Hanako-san desu.

Am I Japanese, American or Canadian?

Anata wa _____ -jin desu.

Am I a teacher? A student?

Anata wa _____ desu.

2. Who am I?

Anata wa _____ *-kun desu.*

Am I Japanese, American or Canadian?

Anata wa _____-jin desu.

Am I a teacher? A student?

Anata wa _____ desu.

Exercise 2

When addressing the people below, what do you put after each of their names? Write **chan**, **san**, **kun** or **sensei** in the blanks.

1. Mr. Kelly, your school teacher

Kelly- _____

2. Hiroshi, a 12-year old boy

Hiroshi- _____

3. Noriko, a 5 year old girl

Noriko- _____

4. Dr. Nakamura, your physician

Nakamura- _____

This, That, and (That) Over There: Kore, Sore and Are

You know how to address other people. The next step is to introduce and talk about other people. To do that, you need to learn pronouns such as *this* and *that* so that you are able to say sentences like *This is Tom* and *That is Helen*.

While the English language has only *this* and *that*, Japanese has three words: **kore**, **sore**, and **are**.

this	**kore**	indicates a thing/person near the speaker.
that	**sore**	indicates a thing/person near the listener.
that	**are**	indicates a thing/person away from the speaker and the listener.

This is Mr. Smith.	**Kore wa Smith-san desu.**
This is Hanako.	**Kore wa Hanako-san desu.**

When you refer to other people to whom you have to show your respect, such as teachers, medical doctors or elders, you use **kochira**, **sochira** and **achira**.

this	**kochira**	*a person near the speaker*
that	**sochira**	*a person near the listener*
that	**achira**	*a person away from the speaker and the listener*

Exercise 3

From the point of view of the teacher in the drawing below, label the chalkboard, pencil and book with the appropriate pronouns.

1. _____

2. _____

3. _____

This is (My) Family

To introduce your family, use the following vocabulary. These words mean "*my* family", and "*my* father", etc., unless otherwise specified.

family	*kazoku*		
grandfather	*ojīsan*	grandmother	*obāsan*
father	*otōsan*	mother	*okāsan*
older (elder) brother	*onisan*	older (elder) sister	*onēsan*
younger brother	*otōto*	younger sister	*imōto*
uncle	*ojisan*	aunt	*obasan*

This is (my) father.	**Kore wa otōsan desu.**
(My) father is a teacher.	**Otōsan wa sensei desu.**
This is (my) younger brother.	**Kore wa otōto desu.**
(My) youger brother is a student.	**Otōto wa gakusei desu.**

Talking About Family

Japanese has two distinct words for brother and two for sister meaning "older brother" and "younger brother", "older sister" and "younger sister". In the Japanese culture, it is important to distinguish whether a brother/sister is older or younger than yourself since anyone older than you is respected automatically. That is why **san** is a part of words for **ojīsan, otōsan, onīsan, ojisan, obāsan, okāsan, onēsan** and **obasan** while **boku, watashi, otōto** and **imōto** do not have **san** in them.

When a Japanese person talks to or refers to an older person in the family, that older person is called as **ojīsan, otōsan, onīsan,** and so on, but the younger family member is referred to or called by their name without **san** after it.

Husband and Wife

Japanese has different words for wife and husband, depending on whose husband and whose wife, as may be seen below.

🔘 my wife   **kanai**
    my husband   **shujin**
    somebody else's wife   **okusan**
    somebody else's husband   **goshujin**

Both **shujin** and **goshujin** mean *master* as well as *husband*.

Exercise 4

🔘 Listen to Tom as he introduces a member of his family. Answer the questions in English.

1. Whom did Tom introduce? _____

2. Whom did Tom introduce? _____

3. Whom did Tom introduce? _____

Exercise 5

🔘 Listen to the track for Exercise 4 again, and fill in the blanks with the correct words in rōmaji.

1. What does Tom's father do? Otōsan wa _____ desu.

2. What does Tom's mother do? _____ wa _____ desu.

3. What nationality is Tom's mother? _____ wa _____ desu.

4. Are Tom and his brother Ken both students? Yes, _____
    to _____ wa gakusei desu.

5. How do you know that Ken is older than Tom? Ken wa
    _____ desu.

Animals

animals	**dōbutsu**		
duck	**ahiru**	squirrel	**risu**
pig	**buta**	monkey	**saru**
snake	**hebi**	badger	**tanuki**
dog	**inu**	tiger	**tora**
giraffe	**kirin**	bird	**tori**
bear	**kuma**	horse	**uma**
cat	**neko**	rabbit	**usagi**
mouse, rat	**nezumi**	cow	**ushi**
lion	**raion**	elephant	**zō**

This is a cow.	**Kore wa ushi desu.**
That is a dog.	**Sore wa inu desu.**
That (over there) is a cat.	**Are wa neko desu.**
These are a dog and a cat.	**Kore wa inu to neko desu.**

This, That and (That) Over There For Places: Koko, Soko and Asoko

Unlike English, Japanese has many different words for *this* and *that*. When you talk about a thing or person, you use **kore**, **sore** and **are** (or **kochira, sochira** and **achira**). When you talk about *this* and *that* related to a place, you must use **koko, soko** and **asoko**.

this (place)	**koko**	*a place near the speaker*
that (place)	**soko**	*a place near the listener*
that (place over there)	**asoko**	*a place away from both the speaker and the listener*

27

Exercise 6

🔊 Imagine yourself visiting a zoo. Listen to the descriptions, and answer the following in English.

1. What animals are nearby? _____

2. What animal is in the distance? _____

3. What animal is very far away? _____

💿 **Places**

Use any of these words in the sentence structure
_ **wa** _ **desu** to describe location.

bus stop	**basu-sutoppu**	kindergarten	**yōchien**
		post office	**yūbinkyoku**
hospital	**byōin**	kitchen	**daidokoro**
department store	**depāto**	bathroom	**furoba**
		family room	**ima**
zoo	**dōbutsuen**	garden	**niwa**
(railway) station	**eki**	washroom (polite)	**otearai**
school	**gakkō**	washroom	**toire**
bank	**ginkō**	apartment	**apāto**
airport	**hikōjō**	house, home	**ie**
hotel	**hoteru**	high-class apartment	**manshon**
bookstore	**hon-ya**	house, home	**uchi**
shrine	**jinja**	river	**kawa**
park	**kōen**	lake	**mizūmi**
toy shop	**omocha-ya**	sea	**umi**
restaurant	**resutoran**	mountain	**yama**
Japanese inn	**ryokan**		
temple	**(o)tera**		

This (place) is a department store.   **Koko wa depāto desu.**

That (place) is a zoo.   **Soko wa dōbutsuen desu.**

That (place over there) is a (railway) station.   **Asoko wa eki desu.**

Write the correct pronoun in the blanks: **kore, sore, are, koko, soko** or **asoko**.

1. To describe the cat you are holding:

_____ wa neko desu.

2. To describe the station you are in:

_____ wa eki desu.

3. To describe the dog near you, but not too close:

_____ wa inu desu.

4. To describe the toilet near you, but not too close:

_____ wa toire desu.

5. To describe the horse far away from you:

_____ wa uma desu.

6. To describe the airport far away from you:

_____ wa hikōjō desu.

Translate into English:

1. Watashi wa Hanako desu. _____

2. Kore wa Amy-san desu. _____

3. Kore wa neko desu. _____

4. Are wa imōto to otōto desu. _____

5. Are wa sensei desu. _____

Translate into rōmaji:

6. I am Betty. _____

7. We are students. _____

8. This is (my) mother. _____

9. These are pigs and cows. _____

10. Betty is (my) younger sister. _____

Exercise 7

Exercise 8

🔘 Introduce the following people/buildings/animals, using the sentence structure _ **wa** _ **desu**. Say each sentence aloud. Check your sentences against the correct answers recorded on the CD.

1. Your younger sister who is beside you _____

2. Your older sister who is near you _____

3. Your father who is far away _____

4. The cat you are holding _____

5. The bird in the sky _____

6. The bank we are in _____

7. The mountain far away _____

Sitting

When you sit in a **tatami** room, different positions are proper for formal and informal situations (see the photos). If a woman sits in any other style than these, for example if she crosses her legs or stretches her legs out, Japanese people will think that she is rude.

Woman's formal sitting pose.   Woman's informal sitting pose.   Man's formal sitting pose.   Man's informal sitting pose.

For each Japanese character, there is a standard order in which the different parts of the character should be drawn, as well as a standard way of drawing each part. For the writing exercises in this book, follow the boxes from left to right for the order of the strokes. There are three basic rules for each part of a character:

1. If the part is vertical or nearly vertical, it is drawn from top to bottom.
2. If the part is horizontal or nearly horizontal, it is drawn from left to right.
3. If, the part is strongly curved, it is usually drawn from the higher end to the lower end.

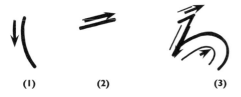

(1)   (2)   (3)

Remember that once you start to draw part of a character, you continue it until the end of that part.

Practice the five hiragana characters **a, i, u, e, o**:
あ， い， う， え， and お.

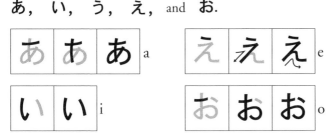

5 Asking and Answering Questions

💿 Dialogue 1

Hanako:	(Anata wa) Tom-kun desu ka.
Tom:	Hai sō desu. Anata wa (dare desu ka).
Hanako:	(Watashi wa) Hanako desu.
	Dōzo yoroshiku.
Tom:	Dōzo yoroshiku.
Hanako:	(Anata wa) Kanada-jin desu ka.
Tom:	Iie (boku wa) Kanada-jin de wa arimasen.
	(Boku wa) Amerika-jin desu.
Hanako:	(Kore wa) chizu desu.
	Amerika wa doko desu ka.
Tom:	(Amerika wa) koko desu.

chizu map

Are You a Canadian?

This is Tom's first day at his new college. He meets Hanako, who is very eager to make conversation.

Hanako:	Are you Tom?
Tom:	Yes, I am. And you are?
Hanako:	I'm Hanako.
	Pleased to meet you.
Tom:	Pleased to meet you too.
Hanako:	Are you a Canadian?
Tom:	No, I am not a Canadian.
	I'm an American.
Hanako:	This is a map.
	Where is America?
Tom:	America is here (this place).

💿 Dialogue 2

Tom:	Konnichiwa.
Hanako:	Konnichiwa. Dōzo .

***

Tom:	(Kore wa) purezento desu.
Hanako:	Arigatō. (Kore wa) nan desu ka.
Tom:	(Kore wa) sakuranbo desu.

***

Hanako:	Kore wa kazoku desu.
Tom:	(Kore wa) okāsan desu ka.
Hanako:	Iie (sore wa) okāsan de wa arimasen.
	(Sore wa) onēsan desu.
	Onēsan wa gakusei desu.
Tom:	(Kore wa) imōto-san desu ka.
Hanako:	Hai (sore wa) imōto desu.
Tom:	Namae wa* (nan desu ka).
Hanako:	(Namae wa) Mari desu.
Tom:	Koko wa doko desu ka.
Hanako:	(Soko wa) kōen desu.

namae	name
purezento	present

This Is (My) Family

Tom visits Hanako with a present.

Tom:	Good afternoon.
Hanako:	Good afternoon. Please (come in).

Tom takes his shoes off and enters the family room.

Tom:	This is a present (for you).
Hanako:	Thank you. What is it?
Tom:	These are cherries.

*See note, page 34

Hanako shows Tom her family photograph.

Hanako:	This is (my) family.
Tom:	Is this (your) mother?
Hanako:	No, that's not (my) mother.
	That's (my) older sister.
	(My) older sister is a student.
Tom:	Is this (your) younger sister?
Hanako:	Yes, it is.
Tom:	What's (her) name?
Hanako:	(Her) name is Mari.
Tom:	Where is this (place)?
Hanako:	That (place) is a park.

🔊 Asking Questions

In Japanese, the particle **ka** at the end of a statement converts it into a question; no question mark is used. **Ka** is pronounced with slightly higher pitch.

This is tempura.	**Kore wa tenpura desu.**
Is this tempura?	**Kore wa tenpura desu ka.**
You are Makoto.	**Anata wa Makoto-kun desu.**
Are you Makoto?	**Anata wa Makoto-kun desu ka.**
This (place) is a (railway) station.	**Koko wa eki desu.**
Is this (place) a (railway) station?	**Koko wa eki desu ka.**

* When an interrogative sentence is abbreviated and **ka** is omitted, the last syllable of the last word is pronounced with slightly higher pitch, to denote that it is a question.

Yes and No: *Hai* and *Iie*

To answer questions, use *yes* or *no*.

hai yes   **iie** no

Now, you may answer questions as follows.

Hai kore wa   Yes, this is tempura.
tenpura desu.

Iie kore wa   No, this is yakitori.
yakitori desu.

Quite often, people abbreviate replies by saying just **hai sō desu,** which should be translated accordingly.

Anata wa Tom-kun desu ka.	Are you Tom?
Hai sō desu.	Yes, I am.
Asoko wa eki desu ka.	Is that the station?
Hai sō desu.	Yes, it is.
Are wa Hanako-san desu ka.	Is that Hanako?
Hai sō desu.	Yes, that is.

Hai

When you are talking to a Japanese person, you will probably hear **hai** after almost every sentence you speak. If you think that he/she is agreeing with you about everything, you are probably mistaken. **Hai** in this case *I am hearing you*. Some people may nod or utter approving sounds instead of saying **hai**.

Exercise 1

🔘 You will hear a statement in Japanese. Convert it into a question and say it back. Check your replies against the answers recorded on the CD. Then translate the questions into English and write them below.

1. _____

2. _____

3. _____

4. _____

5. _____

🔘 Negative Statements

A negative statement for <u>subject</u> **wa** <u>complement</u> **desu** is

<u>subject</u> **wa** <u>complement</u> **de wa arimasen**.

This is a pencil.	**Kore wa enpitsu desu.**
This is not a pencil.	**Kore wa enpitsu de wa arimasen.**
Are you Makoto?	**Anata wa Kakoto-kun desu ka.**
No, I am not Makoto.	**Iie boku wa Makoto-kun de wa arimasen.**
I am Hiroshi.	**Boku wa Hiroshi desu.**
Is this (place) Tokyo?	**Koko wa Tōkyō desu ka.**
No, this (place) is not Tokyo.	**Iie koko wa Tōkyō de wa arimasen.**
This (place) is Nagoya.	**Koko wa Nagoya desu.**

Listen to the statements. Convert what you hear into negative statements and check your answers on the CD.

Translate into English:

1. Sumimasen. Koko wa yūbinkyoku desu ka.

_____

Iie koko wa yūbinkyoku de wa arimasen.

_____

Koko wa ginkō desu.

_____

2. Tom-kun wa Furansu-jin desu ka.

_____

Iie Tom-kun wa Furansu-jin de wa arimasen.

_____

Tom-kun wa Amerika-jin desu.

_____

Translate into rōmaji:

3. Are you Amy?_____

No, I am not Amy. _____

I am Betty. _____

4. Are you an American? _____

No, I am not an American._____

I am a German. _____

*Interrogative Pronouns**

who	**dare**	where, which place	**doko**
which one	**dore**	what	**nan**

By replacing nouns with interrogative pronouns for simple statements, you may convert them into questions. Let's suppose that you want to make the sentence *What is this?* Start by considering one possible answer to the question "*What is this?*"

Start with the statement:	**Kore wa hon desu.**	This is a book.
Since *What is this?* is a question, put **ka** at the end.	**Kore wa hon desu ka.**	Is this a book?
Since **hon** is what you are asking about and it is a "thing," replace **hon** with **nan**, *what*:	**Kore wa nan desu ka.**	What is this?

Now you can go one step further.

What is this?   **Kore wa nan desu ka.**

Replace **kore** with **tenpura** to get:

What is tempura?   **Tenpura wa nan desu ka.**

By changing **nan**, *what*, to **dore,** *which one*, in the above sentence, you get:

Which one is tempura?	**Tenpura wa dore desu ka.**

---

* Japanese grammar classifies **dare** as a pronoun and **nan** as a demonstrative pronoun. We have followed the classification of English grammar.

Let's do the same thing with another sentence, using **dare**, *who*. **Dare** replaces a "person" as follows:

You are Makoto.	**Anata wa Makoto-kun desu.**
Are you Makoto?	**Anata wa Makoto-kun desu ka.**
Who are you?	**Anata wa dare desu ka.**
Who is the teacher?	**Sensei wa dare desu ka.**

Let's try one more example using the question word **doko**, *where*. **Doko** replaces a "place" as follows:

This (place) is a post office.	**Koko wa yūbinkyoku desu.**
Is this (place) a post office?	**Koko wa yūbinkyoku desu ka.**
Where is this (place)?	**Koko wa doko desu ka.**
Where is the toilet?	**Toire wa doko desu ka.**

Listen to the questions and look at the picture. Reply to each question aloud in a full sentence and write it below.

1. _____

2. _____

3. _____

(1)	**(2)**	**(3)**
		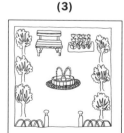

Exercise 5

Look at the pictures above and:
a. Make a statement by writing rōmaji in the blank.
b. Make the statement into a question.
c. Write **nan/dare/doko** in the blank to ask what/who/where.

1. a. Kore wa _____ desu. This is (my) grandmother.

b. Kore wa _____ desu ka. Is this (my) grandmother?

c. Kore wa _____ desu ka. Who is this?

2. a. Kore wa _____ desu. This is a carrot.

b. Kore wa _____ desu ka. Is this a carrot?

c. Kore wa _____ desu ka. What is this?

3. a. Koko wa _____ desu. This is a park.

b. Koko wa _____ desu ka. Is this a park?

c. Koko wa _____ desu ka. Where is this?

Exercise 6

Listen to the statements and questions on the CD, and answer below in rōmaji.

1. _____

2. _____

3. _____

4. _____

🔊 Say the following sentences aloud in Japanese. Check your answers on the CD.

1. What is this (beside me)?

2. What is that (near you)?

3. What is that (far away)?

4. Who is this (beside me)?

5. Who is that (near you)?

6. Who is that (far away)?

7. Where is this place (we are in)?

8. Where is that place?

9. Where is that place (far away)?

Translate into English:

1. Are wa nan desu ka. _____

Are wa hon desu. _____

2. Koko wa doko desu ka. _____

Koko wa kōen desu. _____

3. Ie wa doko desu ka. _____

Translate into rōmaji:

4. Who is that (over there)? _____

That (over there) is a teacher. _____

5. Where is this (place)? _____

This is a department store. _____

6. Who are you? _____

I am Peter. _____

Exercise 9

🔘 You will hear some questions about Dialogue 2. Reply to the questions aloud in Japanese, in full sentences. Check your answers on the CD.

Personal Seals

In Japan, people do not sign their names as in the West. Instead, they use personal seals, which have exactly the same significance as a signature. Every time you want to withdraw or deposit money at a bank, you must use your personal seal.

Writing Exercise

Practice the five hiragana characters *ka, ki, ku, ke* and *ko.*

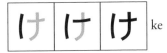

か, き, く, け and こ

か か か ka

け け け ke

き き き ki

こ こ ko

く ku

Is it Yours or Mine?

🔵 Dialogue 1

Hanako: (Kore wa) watashi no (nōto) desu
            (Kore wa) anata no (nōto) desu ka.
Tom: Iie (sore wa) boku no (nōto) de wa arimasen.
            (Sore wa) Makoto-kun no (nōto) desu.

Is This Yours?

Tom and Hanako sort through a pile of notebooks to find theirs.

Hanako: This is mine.
            Is this yours?
Tom: No, it's not mine.
            It's Makoto's.

🔵 The Pencil is Mine

Here is some new vocabulary that you'll use in this lesson.

pencil	**enpitsu**	eyeglasses	**megane**
book	**hon**	wallet/	**saifu**
notebook	**nōto**	purse	
pen	**pen**	chair	**isu**
handbag	**handobaggu**	table	**tēburu**
briefcase	**kaban**	desk	**tsukue**
umbrella	**kasa**		

The Particle No

possessor **no** item possesed

The idea of possessive adjective (*my* of "*my* book", *your* of "*your* pencil") is expressed by using the personal pronoun (**watashi**, **anata**, etc.) followed by **no**.

Thus **Hanako-san no hon** is equivalent to *Hanako's book*. It may be easier to think that **no** has the same function as *'s* in English.

Tom's book	**Tom no hon**
my book	**watashi no hon**
your book	**anata no hon**
my father	**watashi no otōsan**
your father	**anata no otōsan**

The possessors may be not only personal pronouns; they may be nouns, such as *father*, *mother*, *dog*, etc.

father's chair	**otōsan no isu**
mother's chair	**okāsan no isu**
dog's chair	**inu no isu**

Exercise 1

🔘 Say the following phrases aloud in Japanese. Check your answers on the CD.

1. my book

2. your book

3. (my) younger brother's book

4. my father

5. your father

6. Tom's father

Using **No** *to Describe Locations*

name of a place **no** noun

No between two nouns can also express something other than possession. If the first noun is a name of a place, it describes the origin or location of the second noun.
In other words, **no** makes the "place," which is a noun, into an adjective. Here are some countries and cities that you could use in this sentence structure.

countries	**kuni**	Japan	**Nippon**
China	**Chūgoku**	abroad	**gaikoku**
Germany	**Doitsu**	capitals	**shuto**
France	**Furansu**	Washington	**Washinton**
Britain	**Igirisu**	Paris	**Pari**
Italy	**Itaria**	London	**Rondon**
Canada	**Kanada**	Tokyo	**Tōkyō**
Japan	**Nihon**		

Italian handbag	**Itaria no handobaggu**
Japanese apple	**Nihon no ringo**
Tokyo station	**Tōkyō no eki**
London airport	**Rondon no hikōjō**

Using **No** *to Describe Nouns*

A (noun) **no** B (noun)

No is also used between two nouns where the first noun describes the second. In this case, the first noun is neither a person nor a place, and **A no B** is translated as

B of / for / in / on A.

school teacher (teacher of school)	**gakkō no sensei**
book on sports	**supōtsu no hon**

45

💿 Dialogue 2

Hanako: (Kore wa) anata no (hon) desu ka.
Tom: Hai (sore wa) boku no (hon) desu.
Hanako: (Kore wa) Eigo no hon desu ka.
Tom: Iie (sore wa) Eigo no hon de wa arimasen.
           (Sore wa) Furansu-go no hon desu.

Is It a Book in English?

Tom and Hanako are going through a pile of books to find Tom's book.

Hanako: Is this yours?
Tom: Yes, it's mine.
Hanako: Is it a book in English?
Tom: No, it's not a book in English.
           It's a book in French.

-Go: Describing Languages

The suffix **-go** is added to the name of a country for its language (just as **-jin** is used for its people), e.g., **Furansu-go**, *French language*. There are exceptions to the rule such as **Eigo**, *English*.

German language	**Doitsu-go**
English language	**Eigo**
French language	**Furansu-go**
Italian language	**Itaria-go**
Japanese language	**Nihon-go**
Japanese language student	**Nihon-go no gakusei**

(student of the Japanese language)

English language school   **Eigo no gakkō**
(school for the English language)

English book   **Eigo no hon**
(book in the English language)

Using No More Than Once

No can be used more than once in a sentence:

watashi no Eigo no hon
> Consider **eigo no hon** first. It means *an English book*.
> Then consider **watashi no** *English book*: *my English book*.

watashi no gakkō no sensei
> Consider **watashi no gakkō** first. It means *my school*.
> Then consider *my school* **no sensei**: *teacher of my school*.

watashi no otōsan no hon
> Consider **watashi no otōsan** first. It means *my father*.
> Then consider *my father* **no hon**: *my father's book*.

Koko wa watashi no sensei no ie desu.
This (place) is my teacher's house.

⬤ Listen to the
phrases in the CD.
Repeat the
Japanese, then
write the English
translation to the
right.

1. teacher's pen

2. _____

3. _____

4. _____

5. _____

6. _____

Exercise 2

Write rōmaji in the blanks to translate the following phrases.

1. Hanako's sister: Hanako-san no imōto

2. our table: _____ no _____

3. Tom's country: _____ no _____

4. British capital: _____ no _____

5. magazine in the English language:

_____ no _____

6. books on food: _____ no _____

Exercise 3

Dialogue 3

Hanako:	(Kore wa) dare no megane desu ka.
Tom:	(Kore wa boku no) okāsan no (megane) desu.
	(Kore wa) Itaria no (megane) desu.
Hanako:	Kore wa nan no hon desu ka.
Tom:	(Kore wa) kudamono no hon desu.
	(Kore wa) okāsan no (hon) desu.

Whose Eyeglasses Are These?

Hanako visits Tom's house and sees many things that interest her on a table.

Hanako:	Whose eyeglasses are these?
Tom:	They're my mother's.
	They're Italian.
Hanako:	What kind of book is this?
Tom:	It's a book on fruit.
	It's my mother's.

Interrogatives + No

You can ask more questions using the interrogative pronouns **dare**, *who*; **nan**, *what* and **doko**, *where*. Let's suppose that you want to make the sentence *Whose book is this?* Remember to make interrogative sentences by starting with a simple statement and changing it into a question. To do this, consider a simple statement that could be an answer to the question *Whose book is this?*

You start with the statement:	**Kore wa watashi no hon desu.**	This is my book.
Put **ka** at the end to form a question:	**Kore wa watashi no hon desu ka.**	Is this my book?

▶

Since **watashi** is a "person", replace it with **dare**, *who*.

Kore wa dare no hon desu ka.

Whose book is this?

Let's do the same thing with another sentence, using **nan**, *what (kind of)*. **Nan** replaces a "thing".

Kore wa Eigo no hon desu. This is an English book.

Kore wa Eigo no hon desu ka. Is this an English book?

<u>Replace **Eigo** with **nan** to get:</u>

Kore wa nan no hon desu ka. What (kind of) book is this?

Let's try one more example using the question word **doko**, *where*. **Doko** replaces a "place" as follows:

Koko wa Tōkyō no eki desu. This is Tokyo station.

Koko wa Tōkyō no eki desu ka. Is this Tokyo station?

<u>Replace **Tōkyō** with **doko** to get:</u>

Koko wa doko no eki desu ka. Which station is this ?

Listen to the various replies to the question: **Kore wa dare no hon desu ka**. Write down whose book it is in English.

1. <u>father's</u>

2. _____

3. _____

4. _____

5. _____

Exercise 4

Exercise 5

Write **wa, o, ka, to** or **ni** in the blanks, and translate the sentences into English.

1. Koko _____ gakkō desu.   This is a school.

2. Koko _____ gakkō desu ka. _____

3. Koko _____ anata _____ gakkō desu ka. _____

_____

4. Koko _____ anata _____ onēsan _____ gakkō

desu ka._____

5. Pen _____ kudasai. _____

6. Pen _____ enpitsu _____ kudasai.

May I have a pen and a pencil please?

7. Pen _____ enpitsu _____ kudasai.

May I have a pen or a pencil please?

Exercise 6

Write **nan, doko** or **dare** in the blanks so that the replies are appropriate.

1. Question: Koko wa _____ no shuto desu ka.

Reply: Koko wa Chūgoku no shuto desu.

2. Question: Kore wa _____ no handobaggu desu ka.

Reply: Kore wa onēsan no handobaggu desu.

3. Question: Kore wa _____ no shashin desu ka.

Reply: Kore wa Itaria no isu no shashin desu.

Exercise 7

Translate into English:

1. Sensei no isu _____

2. Okāsan no saifu _____

3. Hanako-san no otōsan _____

4. Kore wa watashi no okāsan desu. _____

5. Sore wa watashi-tachi no inu desu. _____

6. Koko wa doko no kuni desu ka. _____

Koko wa Itaria desu. _____

Translate into rōmaji:

7. My Friend _____

8. Your family _____

9. This is (my) mother's umbrella. _____

10. May I have my notebook please? _____

_____

11. I am a student of the English language. _____

_____

12. What kind of fruit is this? _____

This is a watermelon. _____

Practice the five hiragana characters *sa, shi, su, se* and *so.*

さ, し, す, せ and そ.

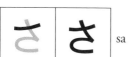

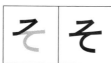 se

 shi

 so

す sa

su

Focus on Action: Verbs

 Dialogue 1

Tom:	(Hanako-san wa) nani o nomimasu ka.
Hanako:	(Watashi wa) orenji-jūsu o nomimasu.
	(Tom-kun wa) nani o nomimasu ka.
Tom:	(Boku wa) tomato-jūsu o nomimasu.
	(Anata wa) nani o tabemasu ka.
Hanako:	(Watashi wa) tenpura o tabemasu.
Tom:	Tenpura wa niku desu ka.
	(Tenpura wa) sakana desu ka.
Hanako:	(Tenpura wa) sakana desu.
Tom:	Boku wa karēraisu to pan o tabemasu.

What Will You Drink?

Tom and Hanako look at the show window of a restaurant to decide what to order.

Tom:	What will you drink?
Hanako:	I'll drink orange juice.
	What will you drink?
Tom:	I'll drink tomato juice.
	What will you eat?
Hanako:	I'll eat tempura.
Tom:	Is tempura meat
	or (is it) fish?
Hanako:	It is fish.
Tom:	I'll eat Indian curry and bread.

V•Masu-Verbs

Japanese verbs can be separated into two groups: **desu** and **V•masu**-verbs. **V•masu**-verbs are a verb form + an auxillary verb **masu**. They are used for the polite style of speech, which is the most commonly used style and the one you should use. Below is a list of **V•masu**-verbs. You will notice that every verb ends in **masu**. The verbs listed below are transitive verbs (verbs which may have direct objects).

wash	*araimasu*	learn	*naraimasu*
speak	*hanashimasu*	drink	*nomimasu*
buy	*kaimasu*	send	*okurimasu*
write, draw	*kakimasu*	eat	*tabemasu*
listen to, hear, ask for	*kikimasu*	take	*torimasu*
		make	*tsukurimasu*
		sell	*urimasu*
see, watch	*mimasu*	read	*yomimasu*

Nouns

Since these are transitive verbs, you need to learn nouns that may be direct objects.

drinks	**nomimono**	wine	**wain**
Japanese green tea	**(o)cha**	candy	**ame**
Indian tea	**kōcha**	candy, sweet	**okashi**
milk	**miruku**	meat	**niku**
water	**mizu**	pork	**buta-niku**
Japanese rice wine	**sake**	beef	**gyū-niku**

chicken (meat)	**tori-niku**	letter	**tegami**
		magazine	**zasshi**
fish	**sakana**	picture, painting	**e**
voice, cry	**koe**		
music	**ongaku**	movie	**eiga**
radio	**rajio**	television	**terebi**
song	**uta**	direction	**hōkō**
newspaper	**shinbun**	stamp	**kitte**

Forming Sentences

A transitive ***V•masu***-verb has the sentence structure:

<u>subject</u> ***wa*** <u>direct object</u> ***o V•masu***

I wash a dog.	***Watashi wa inu o araimasu.***
A dog sees a cat.	***Inu wa neko o mimasu.***
The younger brother eats an apple.	***Otōto wa ringo o tabemasu.***
Mother writes a letter.	***Okāsan wa tegami o kakimasu.***
Father reads a newspaper.	***Otōsan wa shinbun o yomimasu.***
The dog drinks water.	***Inu wa mizu o nomimasu.***
Father buys a newspaper.	***Otōsan wa shinbun o kaimasu.***
I learn English.	***Watashi wa Eigo o naraimasu.***
The younger sister makes bread.	***Imōto wa pan o tsukurimasu.***

A Japanese verb may be translated into more than one verb in English, and vice versa. For instance, ***kikimasu*** may be translated as *hear*, *ask for* and *listen to* as follows.

I hear a bird's cry.	***Watashi wa tori no koe o kikimasu.***
I ask for directions.	***Watashi wa hōkō o kikimasu.***
I listen to the music.	***Watashi wa ongaku o kikimasu.***

Say the
following sentences
aloud in Japanese,
and check your
answers on the CD

1. I eat fish.
2. I drink milk.
3. I speak English.
4. I read newspapers.
5. I buy candy.
6. I listen to the music.
7. I learn Japanese.

Exercise 1

Listen to the phrases and write, in English, who does what.

1. _____

2. _____

3. _____

4. _____

5. _____

6. _____

7. _____

Exercise 2

Sake

When you drink sake with other
people, you do not pour your own
drink. Pour your companions'
drinks, and they will return the favor.

What and What: Nan and Nani

To ask questions using **V•masu**-verbs, just as with **desu**, add the particle **ka** at the end of the statement.

You eat an apple.	**Anata wa ringo o tabemasu.**
Do you eat an apple?	**Anata wa ringo o tabemasu ka.**

The next step is to ask questions such as *What do you eat?*, *What do you drink?*, and *What do you read?*
For *what*, **nan** is used before a word starting with *n/d/t*, and **nani** is used before a word starting with any other letter.

Is this a book?	**Kore wa hon desu ka.**
What is this?	**Kore wa nan desu ka.**
Is this an English book?	**Kore wa Eigo no hon desu ka.**
What (kind of) book is this?	**Kore wa nan no hon desu ka.**

Notice that **nan** comes before **desu** and **no**.

Do you buy apples?	**Anata wa ringo o kaimasu ka.**
What do you buy?	**Anata wa nani o kaimasu ka.**
What do you drink?	**Anata wa nani o nomimasu ka.**
What do you eat?	**Anata wa nani o tabemasu ka.**

Notice that **nani** comes before **o**.

You may add suffixes such as **-jin**, *people*, and **-go**, *language*, to produce **nani-jin**, *what nationality*, and **nani-go**, *what language*.

Write either **nan** or **nani** in the blanks and then
translate the sentences into English.

1. Anata wa _____no niku o tabemasu ka.

What meat do you eat?

2. Anata wa _____ -go o hanashimasu ka.

_____

3. Anata wa _____ o nomimasu ka.

_____

Translate into English:

1. Watashi wa terebi o mimasu. _____

2. Watashi to otōto wa Nihon-go o naraimasu.

_____

3. Otōsan wa shinbun to zasshi o yomimasu.

_____

4. Watashi-tachi wa ongaku o kikimasu. _____

_____

5. Anata wa Nihon-go o hanashimasu ka. _____

_____

6. Anata wa nani o tabemasu ka. _____

_____

7. Anata wa nan no hon o yomimasu ka. _____

_____

8. Anata wa nani o kaimasu ka. _____

_____

9. Anata wa nani o tsukurimasu ka. _____

_____

▶

Translate into rōmaji:

10. We read Japanese books. _____

11. We learn English. _____

12. I listen to Japanese music. _____

_____

13. Does your father drink sake? _____

_____

14. What language do you speak? _____

_____

15. What do you drink? _____

_____

16. What (kind of) fruit do you eat? _____

_____

17. What (kind of) book do you read? _____

_____

18. What movie do you watch? _____

_____

Future Tense

In Japanese, **V•masu**-verbs have the same form for both the
present and future tenses. (This is not the case for **desu**.)
Watashi wa ringo o tabemasu may be translated as *I eat an
apple* or *I will eat an apple*. There is rarely any confusion as
to which translation to choose because the context usually
makes the tense clear. Vocabulary, such as the words shown
below, may also be used to indicate the future tense.

tomorrow   **ashita**
next year   **rainen**
next week   **rai-shū**

Negative Statements and Questions

🔘 Dialogue 1

Hanako: Amerika no kodomo-tachi wa Nihon-go o naraimasu ka.
Tom: Iie naraimasen.
Hanako: (Amerika no kodomo-tachi wa) nani o naraimasu ka.
Tom: (America no kodomo-tachi wa) Eigo to Furansugo to chiri to kagaku to sansū o naraimasu.
Hanako: Amerika-jin wa nani-go o hanashimasu ka.
Tom: (Amerika-jin wa) Eigo o hanashimasu.
Hanako: Amerika-jin wa nani o tabemasu ka.
Tom: (Amerika-jin wa) niku to yasai to pan o tabemasu.

Do American Children Learn Japanese?

Hanako asks Tom about America.

Hanako: Do American children learn Japanese?
Tom: No, they don't.
Hanako: What do they learn?
Tom: They learn English, French, geography, science and arithmetic.
Hanako: What language do Americans speak?
Tom: They speak English.
Hanako: What do Americans eat?
Tom: They eat meat, vegetables and bread.

School Subjects

geography	**chiri**	history	**rekishi**
science	**kagaku**	arithmetic	**sansū**
the national language	**kokugo**	mathematics	**sūgaku**

Negatives

For the verbs ending with *masu*, you can make negative statements by changing *masu* into *masen*.

I wash a dog.	*Watashi wa inu o araimasu.*
I do not wash a dog.	*Watashi wa inu o araimasen.*
(My) younger brother speaks English.	*Otōto wa Eigo o hanashimasu.*
(My) younger brother does not speak English.	*Otōto wa Eigo o hanashimasen.*
Mother makes bread.	*Okāsan wa pan o tsukurimasu.*
Mother does not make bread.	*Okāsan wa pan o tsukurimasen.*

Answering Questions

You can answer a question with *hai* + a positive verb (for a positive reply) or *iie* + a negative verb (for a negative reply).

Question	*Answer*
Anata wa Nihon-go no hon o yomimasu ka.	*Hai yomimasu/ hanashimasu.*
Do you read Japanese books?	Yes, I do.
	or
Anata wa Itaria-go o hanashimasu ka.	*Iie yomimasen/ hanashimasen.*
Do you speak Italian?	No, I don't.

Fill in the table below.

Meaning	Positive verb	Negative verb
read	yomimasu	yomimasen
	torimasu	
sell		
		okurimasen
	nomimasu	

Listen to the speaker describing her younger sister. Answer the following questions in rōmaji, using only **hai** or **iie** and a verb, e.g., **hai tabemasu, iie tabemasen.**

1. Watashi no imōto wa miruku o nomimasu ka._____

2. Watashi no imōto wa (o)-cha o nomimasu ka._____

3. Watashi no imōto wa shinbun o yomimasu ka. _____

4. Watashi no imōto wa Nihon-go o naraimasu ka. _____

5. Watashi no imōto wa terebi o mimasu ka. _____

6. Watashi no imōto wa Eigo o hanashimasu ka. _____

Exercise 3

Translate into English:

1. Boku wa inu o araimasen. _____

2. Onē san wa niku o tabemasen. _____

3. Okā san wa kudamono o kaimasen. _____

_____

4. Imōto wa pan o tsukurimasen. _____

5. Otōto wa otōsan no hon o yomimasen. _____

_____

6. Watashi wa Eigo o hanashimasen. _____

7. Anata wa Doitsu-go o naraimasu ka. Iie naraimasen. _____

_____

Translate into rōmaji:

8. I do not write letters. _____

_____

9. (My) mother does not drink milk. _____

_____

10. Makoto does not eat udon. _____

_____

11. Tom does not read newspapers. _____

_____

12. I do not listen to the music. _____

_____

13. I do not speak Japanese. _____

_____

▶

14. Are you going to buy this? No, I am not. _____

_____

 Dialogue 2

Hanako:	Bideo o mimasen ka.
Tom:	(Bideo wa) nan no bideo desu ka.
Hanako:	(Bideo wa) inu no eiga desu.
	(Eiga wa) Dizunī no manga desu.
	Eiga wa Eigo desu.
Tom:	Hai mimasu.

Dizunī	Disney
manga	comics, cartoon
bideo	video

Would You Like to Watch a Video?

Hanako suggests that Tom watch a video with her.

Hanako:	Would you like to watch a video?
Tom:	What kind of video is it?
Hanako:	It's a movie of a dog.
	It's a Disney cartoon.
	The movie is in English.
Tom:	Yes, I'll watch it.

Would You Like To _?: Negative V•masu + Ka

"Negative **V•masu**-verb + **ka**" means *Would you like to _?* in English. This expression is used primarily in one-to-one conversation, and the subject, which is always the person to whom you are speaking, is usually dropped.

Question	*Answer*
Eiga o mimasen ka.	**Hai mimasu/yomimasu.**
Would you like to see a movie?	Yes, I would.
Kore o yomimasen ka.	*or*
Would you like to read this?	**Iie mimasen/yomimasen.**
	No, I would not.

Exercise 4

The speaker will suggest an activity. Write down the suggestion in English.

1. _____

2. _____

3. _____

4. _____

5. _____

Offering Food: _masen Ka

When the expression *_**masen ka**_* is used with respect to food or drinks, replies are a little tricky. Let us look at the following example in which someone suggests that you drink coffee.

Question

Would you like to drink coffee?   **Kōhī o nomimasen ka.**

Replies

Yes, I would.   **Hai nomimasu.**

No, I would not.   **Iie nomimasen.**

In the example, a speaker suggests coffee without specifying who will provide it. For instance, when you are walking on a street with a friend, he may suggest having a coffee. You do not know whether he is thinking of buying coffee for you, or going Dutch. If that is the case, the above replies are appropriate.

When it is obvious that someone is offering you a coffee, such as when you are in his home, more polite replies are appropriate. You may recall that **itadakimasu**, *thank you*, is the phrase used to accept an offer with gratitude. To refuse with gratitude, use the phrase below.

Yes, thank you.   **Hai itadakimasu.**
(accepting with gratitude)

No, thank you.   **Iie kekkō desu.**
(rejecting with gratitude)

Exercise 5

🔘 Say the following sentences aloud in Japanese and check your answers on the CD.

1. Would you like to drink?

2. Would you like to watch?

3. Would you like to buy?

4. Would you like to learn Japanese?

5. Would you like to eat chow mein?

Exercise 6

Translate into English:

1. Kore o mimasen ka. _____

2. Furansu-go o naraimasen ka. _____

3. Ongaku o kikimasen ka. _____

4. Nihon-go o hanashimasen ka. _____

5. Sushi o tabemasen ka. _____

Hai itadakimasu. _____

6. Mizu o nomimasen ka. _____

Iie kekkō desu. _____

Translate into rōmaji:

7. Would you like to speak English? _____

_____

8. Would you like to draw a picture? _____

_____

9. Would you like to listen to Japanese music? _____

_____

10. Would you like to learn German? _____

_____

11. Would you like to drink Japanese green tea? Yes, thank you.

_____

The School System

The Japanese school system consists of six years of elementary school from ages 7 to 13, three years of secondary school from ages 13 to 16, three years of high school from ages 16 to 19 and four years of university from ages 19 to 23. Elementary schools and secondary schools are compulsory, and enrollment and literacy rates are essentially 100 percent. There are also kindergartens for children of ages 4 to 7, technical colleges instead of high schools, and junior colleges instead of universities. More than 90 percent of secondary school graduates go to high schools.

Japanese society judges people by the schools they attend, and careers depend greatly on the university from which one graduates. Because of this, the competition to get into a good university is fierce. To get into a good university, one has to get into a good high school, and to do that one has to first get into a good secondary school. Even at 10 years old, a child often has to go to a cram school after regular school. He or she hardly has any other free time except to do homework from both schools.

English is taught from secondary school on, and students must get passing grades in English, mathematics and Japanese on the university entrance exam. Once the student gets into a university, graduation is almost guaranteed, so they spend a good part of their time enjoying themselves or working at part-time jobs.

Writing Exercise

Practice the five hiragana characters *ta, chi, tsu, te* and *to*.

た，ち，つ，て and と.

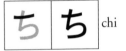 ta 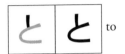 te

ちち chi とと to

つ tsu

Japanese Particles: De

🔵 Dialogue 1

Hanako: Yakisoba o tabemasen ka.
Tom: Hai itadakimasu.
Hanako: (Anata wa yakisoba o) (o)hashi de tabemasu ka.
　　　　Hōku de tabemasu ka.
Tom: (Boku wa yakisoba o) hōku de tabemasu.
Hanako: (Anata wa) nani o (o)hashi de tabemasu ka.
Tom: (Boku wa) sakana o ((o)hashi de) tabemasu.

Do You Eat With Chopsticks or a Fork?

Hanako offers Tom yakisoba.

Hanako: Would you like to eat yakisoba?
Tom: Yes, thank you.
Hanako: Do you eat it with chopsticks or a fork?
Tom: I will eat it with a fork.
Hanako: What do you eat with chopsticks?
Tom: I eat fish.

The Particle De

Using the **V•masu**-verbs you have learned in the previous lesson, you can say many simple sentences such as *I eat an apple, I read a book,* etc. By using the particle **de**, you can expand on those sentences. The particle **de** following a noun has two uses. One is to indicate "how", or "with what instrument", something is done. Translated according to context, it can mean *in/with/by.* Be careful not to confuse this with the "with" of accompaniment (*I go to school with Makoto*).

I wash a dog with water. (with what?)	***Watashi wa inu o mizu de araimasu.***
I wash a dog by hand. (with what?)	***Watashi wa inu o te de araimasu.***
Father writes a letter with a pen. (with what?)	***Otōsan wa tegami o pen de kakimasu.***
Father writes a letter in English. (how?)	***Otōsan wa tegami o Eigo de kakimasu.***

How

To describe the instrument you use to do something, you will often need to mention parts of the body, eating utensils or modes of transportation. The vocabulary below will be useful for describing how or with what instrument you do many things.

body	karada	stomach, abdomen	onaka
leg	ashi		
head	atama	hand	te
nose	hana	arm	ude
hair	kami	finger	yubi
face	kao	chopsticks	hashi
shoulder	kata	fork	hōku
mouth	kuchi	knife	naifu
eye	me	spoon	supūn
ear	mimi	bus	basu

You will hear a Japanese word for a body part. Write the number corresponding to the body part in the correct blank.

De to Describe Place

The second use of **de** is to express "action in a place." Translated according to context, it can mean *in/at/on.*

I wash a dog in the garden	***Watashi wa inu o niwa de arimasu.***
I read a magazine on a bus.	***Watashi wa zasshi o basu de yomimasu.***
Father draws a picture at a mountain.	***Otōsan wa e o yama de kakimasu.***

Exercise 2

Say the following sentences aloud in Japanese. Write your answers below and check your pronunciation on the CD.

1. I write a letter with (my) hand. [not with a computer] _____

_____

2. I write a letter in the garden. _____

3. I write a letter with a pen. _____

4. I write a letter in English. _____

5. I eat steak in the kitchen. _____

6. I eat steak with knife and fork. _____

Exercise 3

Translate into English:

1. Watashi wa udon o (o)hashi de tabemasu. _____

_____

2. Onēsan wa Eigo no uta o rajio de kikimasu. _____

_____

3. Anata wa tegami o nan de kakimasu ka. _____

_____

4. Otōsan wa hon o heya de yomimasu. _____

_____

5. Watashi-tachi wa Eigo o gakkō de naraimasu._____

_____

6. Okāsan wa kudamono o niwa de tsukurimasen._____

_____

7. Ojīsan wa pan o doko de kaimasu ka. _____

_____

Translate into rōmaji:

8. Hanako washes a cat with water. _____

_____

9. We eat meat with knife and fork._____

_____

10. Grandmother reads books with glasses. _____

_____

11. Elephants eat bananas with (their) trunks (noses). _____

_____

12. I do not write a letter in Japanese. _____

_____

13. Do you learn music at school? _____

_____

14. I do not speak Japanese at home. _____

_____

De with the Verb Desu

One of the first things you will do when you get friendly with a Japanese person is to ask for words in Japanese. It's a great way to get acquainted and learn new words.

De is used with the verb **desu** when you want to ask for words in Japanese. Consider **Kore wa nan desu ka**, *What is this?* By inserting **Nihon-go de**, *in Japanese*, you get **Kore wa Nihon-go de nan desu ka**, *What is this in Japanese?*

Similarly, let's consider **Kore wa RINGO desu**, *This is "RINGO".* By inserting **Nihon-go de**, *in Japanese*, you get **Kore wa Nihon-go de RINGO desu**, *This is "RINGO" in Japanese.* By changing **Kore** with APPLE, you get **"APPLE" wa Nihon-go de RINGO desu**, *APPLE is "RINGO" in Japanese.*

What is TOKEI in English?	**TOKEI wa Eigo de nan desu ka.**
It's WATCH.	(**TOKEI wa Eigo de**) **WATCH desu.**
What is SANGURASU in English?	**SANGURASU wa Eigo de nan desu ka.**
It's SUNGLASSES.	(**SANGURASU wa Eigo de**) **SUNGLASSES desu.**

Exercise 4

Translate into English.

1. Kore wa Nihon-go de nan desu ka. _____

_____

2. Kore wa Eigo de nan desu ka. _____

_____

Make sentences by putting appropriate words in the blanks.

1. _____ wa Nihon-go de MIZU desu.

2. ASHI wa Eigo de _____ desu.

3. NEKO wa Eigo de _____ desu.

4. DOG wa Nihon-go de _____ desu.

5. _____ wa Eigo de BOOK desu.

Exercise 5

When you hear a question, reply to it aloud in a full sentence in Japanese. Write your answers below and check your pronunciation on the CD.

1. _____

2. _____

3. _____

4. _____

Exercise 6

Chopsticks and Table Manners

A traditional Japanese meal consists of small servings of many different colorful dishes, all served together on your own tray. Japanese use chopsticks to eat, and food is served in bite-sized pieces which you pick up with your chopsticks. You will never need to cut anything; if there is anything large, you can break it up with your chopsticks.

You use one hand to hold chopsticks and the other hand to pick up bowls and plates, to bring the food closer to your mouth so it does not drop out of your chopsticks.

Never dig chopsticks into rice or any other food. It is regarded as very bad manners: sticking chopsticks into rice is done only when people offer rice to a deceased person at an altar. When you are not using chopsticks, rest the "eating end" on a plate or a chopsticks-rest.

With a buffet style meal, there may be chopsticks on communal plates and bowls for serving. If there are not, eat with one end of your chopsticks and pick food from communal serving plates with the other end.

More Particles: **To, Ne, Yo**

Dialogue 1

Tom: Are wa Kazuko-san desu ne.
Hanako: Iie (are wa) Yōko-san desu yo.
           (Yōko-san wa) Kazuko-san no onēsan desu yo.
           (Yōko-san wa) watashi no onēsan no
           tomodachi desu.

That's Kazuko, Isn't it?

Tom sees a familiar face and asks Hanako who she is.

Tom: That's Kazuko, isn't it?
Hanako: No, that's Yoko!
           Kazuko's older sister!
           She is (my) older sister's friend.

Do You Agree With Me? The Particle Ne

You will often hear **ne** at the end of a sentence. This particle
at the end of a sentence solicits agreement from the listener.
According to context, it can mean *Isn't it?*, *Don't you?*, etc.

That is a book, isn't it?   **Are wa hon desu ne.**

You'll eat an apple, won't   **Anata wa ringo o tabemasu**
you?   **ne.**

Together: The Particle To

When the particle **to** follows a person, it means *together/
along with*.

I watch a movie with Hanako.   **Watashi wa eiga o Hanako-
                                 san to mimasu.**

Would you like to eat lunch   **Ranchi o watashi to**
with me?   **tabemasen ka.**

Pay Attention! The Particle Yo

Yo at the end of a sentence higlights what the speaker is saying. It is similar to an exclamation mark in English.

That is our bus!   *Are wa watashi-tachi no basu desu yo.*

We will eat (meals)!   *Watashi-tachi wa (gohan o) tabemasu yo.*

Exercise 1

🔘 You will hear a sentence. Convert it into a sentence that solicits an agreement from the listener. Say it aloud and write it in rōmaji, then check your answers on the CD.

1. _____

2. _____

3. _____

4. _____

5. _____

Exercise 2

🔘 Say the following sentences aloud in Japanese. Check your answers on the CD.

1. I drink coffee with a friend.

2. I watch TV with my family.

3. I speak Japanese with my older brother.

4. I learn Japanese with my younger brother.

5. I listen to the music with my mother.

Translate into English:

1. Watashi wa ongaku o Makoto-kun to kikimasu._____

_____

2. Sukiyaki o watashi-tachi to tabemasen ka. _____

_____

3. Anata wa Eigo o dare to hanashimasu ka._____

_____

4. Anata wa Hanako-san desu ne. _____

_____

5. Are wa boku-tachi no basu desu yo. _____

_____

Translate into rōmaji:

6. What do you make with Makoto?_____

_____

7. Would you like to watch a video with me? _____

_____

8. I will not speak with Hanako. _____

_____

9. That is the hospital, isn't it? _____

_____

10. This is mine! _____

Word Order in Japanese Sentences

Particles may be separated into three categories, depending on where they appear in sentences.

1. **Ka, ne, yo**: placed at the end of a sentence, after the verb, meaning *?*, *Isn't it?*, *!*.

2. **To, ka, no**: put between words, meaning *and, or,* and in the case of **no,** possessive, *origin of,* or *of/for/in/on.* They always stay between words.

3. **Wa, o, de, to, (ni, ga, e, kara)**: describe and follow nouns/pronouns. They make a noun/pronoun the subject, the direct object, the adverb clause, etc. A "noun/pronoun + its particle" may be put anywhere in a sentence before a verb.

Note that **ka** appears in two different locations for two different purposes in sentences: one for questions at the ends of sentences, and another to mean *or* between words. **To** also appears in two different locations: one between nouns/pronouns meaning *and* and another after nouns/pronouns meaning *with.*

Verbs always come either at the ends of sentences or just before **ka/ne/yo** placed at the ends. Complements, which are not followed by any particle, must come before the verb **desu**.

The following sentences all mean the same thing:

Anata wa inu o niwa de araimasu ka.   Do you wash the

Anata wa niwa de inu o araimasu ka.   dog in the

Inu o anata wa niwa de araimasu ka.   garden?

Inu o niwa de anata wa araimasu ka.

Niwa de anata wa inu o araimasu ka.

Niwa de inu o anata wa araimasu ka.

To make learning easier, we will basically stick to the sentence structure **SUBJECT + DIRECT OBJECT + OTHERS + V•MASU-VERB + KA/NE/YO**. That is, we write *Anata wa inu o niwa de araimasu ka*, rather than any other forms shown above.

Word Order with Desu

Note also that the following sentences are equivalent.
APPLE wa Nihon-go de RINGO desu yo.
Nihon-go de APPLE wa RINGO desu yo.
APPLE is RINGO in Japanese!

You can see that the verb *desu* always comes before the particle *yo (/ka/ne)*. The complement (**RINGO** in the above sentences), which is not followed by any particle, comes before *desu*. The "noun/pronoun + its particle"s (**APPLE wa** and **Nihon-go de**) are interchangable. Just as with **V•masu**-verbs, we will basically keep to the sentence structure **SUBJECT + OTHERS + COMPLEMENT + DESU + KA/NE/YO**.

The following examples show you that "noun/pronoun + *to/ka/no* + noun/pronoun" is treated as one unit (**to/ka/ no**, *and/or of* category 2 on page 80).

Watashi wa <u>inu to neko</u> o araimasu.
<u>Inu to neko</u> o watashi wa araimasu.
I wash the dog and the cat.

Watashi wa <u>otōsan no hon</u> o yomimasen.
<u>Otōsan no hon</u> o watashi wa yomimasen.
I do not read (my) father's book.

Watashi wa terebi o <u>Hanako-san ka Makoto-kun</u> to mimasu.
<u>Hanako-san ka Makoto-kun</u> to watashi wa terebi o mimasu.
I watch TV with Hanako or Makoto.

Exercise 4

Rewrite the following sentences in any different possible orders.

1. Tom-kun wa Nihon-go to Eigo o hanashimasu yo. _____

_____

_____

_____

2. Watashi wa Hanako-san to ranchi o tabemasu._____

_____

_____

_____

3. Anata no namae wa Hanako-san desu ka. _____

_____

_____

_____

Writing Exercise

Practice the five hiragana characters *na, ni, nu, ne* and *no*.

な，に，ぬ，ね and の.

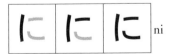

 ne

にににni

のno

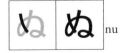 nu

Numbers and Dates

🔘 Dialogue 1

Tom:	Kore wa ikura desu ka.
Clerk:	(Kore wa) go-hyaku kyū-jū-en desu.
Tom:	Kore wa (ikura desu ka).
Clerk:	(Kore wa) roppyaku san-jū-en desu.
Tom:	Kore o kudasai.

How Much Is This?

Tom goes shopping.

Tom:	How much is this?
Clerk:	It's 590 yen.
Tom:	How about this?
Clerk:	It's 630 yen.
Tom:	May I have this please?

Numbers

Japanese uses the same numerals as the West does. So if you do not understand the price a shop clerk tells you, you could always hand him a piece of paper to write it down. Similarly, if you don't know how to say the time and date you want your friend to meet you, you could always write it on a piece of paper. The date is written in year/month/day format, and the time is written as hour:minute. That is, April 23 2006 is written as 2006/04/23 and 25 minutes after 11 o'clock is written as 11:25.

🔊 1 - 1,000,000

The basic numbers are listed below.

0	zero	8	hachi
1	ichi	9	kyū/ku*
2	ni	10	jū
3	san	100	hyaku
4	yon/shi*	1,000	sen
5	go	10,000	man
6	roku	100,000	jū-man
7	nana/shichi*	1,000,000	hyaku-man

Forming Large Numbers

Many-digit numbers are formed the same way in Japanese as they are in English. For instance, *2,457* is expressed as **2 sen** (*thousand*) + **4 hyaku** (*hundred*) + **5 jū** (*ten*) + **7**. The 2, 4 and 5 are called multipliers and the 7 is simply called the last digit. A five digit number is expressed as:

multiplier **-man** + multiplier **-sen** + multiplier **-hyaku** + multiplier **-jū** + last digit

↑ ten thousands   ↑ thousands   ↑ hundreds   ↑ tens   ↑ ones

Some numbers change spelling when **hyaku** and **sen** are combined with multipliers: they are **sanbyaku**, *300*; **roppyaku**, *600*; **happyaku**, *800*; **sanzen**, *3000* and **hassen**, *8000*. The multiplier **ichi**, *1*, is used only for **ichi-man**, *10,000*, and not used for **sen**, *1,000*, **hyaku**, *100* and **jū**, *10*. Hence *11,111* is **ichi-man sen hyaku jū ichi**. You can now say any number from *1* to *1,000,000* in Japanese.

5,263   **go-sen ni-hyaku roku-jū san**

7,928   **nana-sen kyū-hyaku ni-jū hachi**

* Note that 4, 7 and 9 have two forms in Japanese. **Shi**, 4; **shichi**, 9 and **ku**, 9 are not used as multipliers

Exercise 1

⬤ Say the numbers from 1 to 10, and then 100, 1,000, and 10,000 aloud. Check your answers on the CD.

Exercise 2

⬤ You will hear some Japanese telephone numbers. Write them down. Japanese telephone numbers are expressed as "number for the area code – number for the exchange – number." The numbers are said individually; **no** is used for hyphens and **ban**, *number*, is put at the end; 2 and 5 are pronounced as **nī** and **gō** when describing telephone numbers.

1. 072-856-7211

2. _____

3. _____

Translate into English:

Exercise 3

1. ni-sen nana-hyaku san-jū ni _____
_____

2. san-man yon-sen go-hyaku roku-jū hachi _____
_____

3. yon-sen kyu-hyakū hachi-jū ichi_____
_____

Translate into rōmaji:

4. 735 _____

5. 5,241 _____

6. 9,726 _____

Money

Perhaps the most important suffix that is put after a number is the suffix **-en**, which tells an amount of money. **_-en**, written also as **¥_**, is translated as _ yen. For example, **ni-hyaku-en**, ¥200, means 200 yen.

Area where you pay for your purchases.

Ikura: How Much?

Ikura* is used to ask *how much*.

Let's try to make the sentence *How much is this?* Start with the statement **Kore wa ni-hyaku-en desu**, *This is 200 yen.* Put **ka** at the end to form a question, *Is this 200 yen?* Then replace **ni-hyaku-en** with **ikura**, to get **Kore wa ikura desu ka**, *How much is this?*

Exercise 4

You have asked a shop clerk **Kore wa ikura desu ka**, *How much is this?* Listen for the replies. Write down the amount you hear in English.

1. _____ yen

2. _____ yen

3. _____ yen

4. _____ yen

Days and Months

It is very easy to express months in Japanese, just put the suffix *-gatsu* after a number to indicate the month. **Yon**, *4*; **nana**, *7* and **kyū**, *9*, are not used to indicate the months; instead, the alternate forms of 4, 7, and 9 (**shi**, **shichi** and **ku**, respectively) are used. The numbers associated with the month, day, hour and minutes are written without hyphens. That is, instead of **jū-ni**, *12*, **jūni** is used to write **jūni-gatsu**, *December*; instead of **san-jū-ichi**, *31*, **sanjūichi** is used to write **sanjūichi-nichi**, *31st*.

🔘 Months

January	**ichi-gatsu**	July	**shichi-gatsu**
February	**ni-gatsu**	August	**hachi-gatsu**
March	**san-gatsu**	September	**ku-gatsu**
April	**shi-gatsu**	October	**jū-gatsu**
May	**go-gatsu**	November	**jūichi-gatsu**
June	**roku-gatsu**	December	**jūni-gatsu**

Dates

Dates within a month are slightly more complicated, and you must memorize the 1st to the 10th. The suffix *-nichi* is put after the numbers to form the rest of the days of the month except the 14th, 20th and 24th.

▶

1st	tsuitachi	17th	jūshichi-nichi*
2nd	futsuka	18th	jūhachi-nichi
3rd	mikka	19th	jūku-nichi*
4th	yokka	20th	hatsuka
5th	itsuka	21st	nijūichi-nichi
6th	muika	22nd	nijūni-nichi
7th	nanoka	23rd	nijūsan-nichi
8th	yōka	24th	nijūyokka*
9th	kokonoka	25th	nijūgo-nichi
10th	tōka	26th	nijūroku-nichi
11th	jūichi-nichi	27th	nijūshichi-nichi*
12th	jūni-nichi		
13th	jūsan-nichi	28th	nijūhachi-nichi
14th	jūyokka*	29th	nijūku-nichi*
15th	jūgo-nichi	30th	sanjū-nichi
16th	jūroku-nichi	31st	sanjūichi-nichi

*Note that **shi**, *4*; **nana**, *7* and **kyū**, *9*, are not used to indicate dates.

Days of the Week

The days of the week don't follow any rules except that they all carry the suffix -yōbi.

Sunday	nichi-yōbi	Wednesday	sui-yōbi
Monday	getsu-yōbi	Thursday	moku-yōbi
Tuesday	ka-yōbi	Friday	kin-yōbi
		Saturday	do-yōbi

How to Tell a Date

To say the date in Japanese, start with the year, followed by the month, followed by the day of the month, followed by the day of the week. This is written as year/month/date/day of the week. The suffix *–nen*, *year*, is put after a number for the year.

Sen kyū-hyaku kyū-jū kyū-nen go-gatsu nanoka getsu-yōbi
Monday 7 May 1999
Ni-sen ichi-nen san-gatsu itsuka sui-yōbi
Wednesday 5 March 2001

The suffixes associated with dates are summarized below.
-gatsu is put after a number to tell the month.
-nen   is put after a number to tell the year.
-nichi is put after some numbers to tell the date.
-yōbi   denotes the day of the week.

Exercise 5

You will hear the birthday of each of Hanako's family members. Write down the date for each of them in English. The Japanese words for birthday are *(o)tanjōbi/bāsude*.

1. Father's birthday is _____

2. Mother's birthday is _____

3. The older sister's birthday is _____

4. Hanako's birthday is _____

5. The younger sister's birthday is _____

Exercise 6

The following are special dates in Japan. Write and then say the dates of the holidays in Japanese. Check your answers on the CD.

1. 1 January (*(O)shōgatsu*, *New Year's Day*)
<u>Ichigatsu tsuitachi wa (o)shogatsu desu. January 1 is New</u>
<u>Year's Day.</u>

2. 3 March (*Hinamatsuri*, *The Festival of Dolls*, regarded as festival for girls)

_____

3. 5 May (*Kodomo no hi*, *Children's Day*, regarded as festival for boys)

_____

4. 7 July (*Tanabata*, *The Festival of Stars*, celebration of the annual tryst of stars Altair and Vega, separated by the Milky Way)

_____

5. 25 December (*Kurisumasu*, *Christmas*)

_____

6. 31 December (*Ōmisoka*, *New Year's Eve*)

_____

Exercise 7

Translate into English:

1. Ni-sen ni-nen san-gatsu itsuka sui-yōbi

_____

2. Ni-sen-nen roku-gatsu nijūgo-nichi getsu-yōbi

_____

3. Sen kyū-hyaku hachi-jū ichi-nen san-gatsu futsuka do-yōbi

_____

4. Sen nana-hyaku ni-jū roku-nen hachi-gatsu jūku-nichi nichi-yōbi

_____

▶

Translate into rōmaji:

5. Saturday 14 February 2004 _____

_____

6. Wednesday 28 October 1579 _____

_____

7. Sunday 5 July 1400 _____

_____

8. Monday 1 January 2001 _____

_____

Practice the five hiragana characters *ha, hi, fu, he* and *ho*.

は， ひ， ふ， へ　and　ほ.

 ha

ひ hi

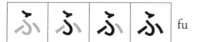 fu

へ he

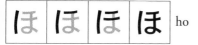 ho

12 Telling Time

Dialogue 1

Tom:	Sumimasen. Ima (wa) nan-ji desu ka.
Clerk:	(Ima wa) hachi-ji nijūgo-fun sugi desu.
Tom:	(Kippu o) Seto made ichi-mai kudasai.
	(Kippu wa) ikura desu ka.
Clerk:	(Kippu wa) yon-hyaku hachi-jū-en desu.
***	
Tom:	(Kore wa) sen-en desu.
Clerk:	(O)tsuri wa go-hyaku ni-jū-en desu.
Tom:	Densha wa nan-ji desu ka.
Clerk:	(Densha wa) ku-ji go-fun desu.
Tom:	Purattohōmu wa doko desu ka.
Clerk:	(Purattohōmu wa) ni-ban sen desu.

densha	electric train
purattohōmu	platform
sen	(train)line
tsuri	change
made	until, till

What Time Is it Now?

Tom buys a train ticket at a station.

Tom:	Excuse me. What time is it now?
Clerk:	It is 25 past 8.
Tom:	May I have 1 ticket to Seto please?
	How much is it?
Clerk:	It is ¥480.

Tom puts money on the money-receiving tray.

Tom:	This is ¥1000.
Clerk:	The change is ¥520.
Tom:	What time is the train?

Clerk:	It's at 9:05.
Tom:	Where is the platform?
Clerk:	It's the (train) line number 2.

Hours

Hours are formed by putting the suffix **-ji** after the numbers, with the exception of **yo-ji**, *four o'clock*, which has gone through a phonetic change (from **yon-ji**).

1 o'clock	**ichi-ji**	7 o'clock	**shichi-ji***
2 o'clock	**ni-ji**	8 o'clock	**hachi-ji**
3 o'clock	**san-ji**	9 o'clock	**ku-ji***
4 o'clock	**yo-ji***	10 o'clock	**jū-ji**
5 o'clock	**go-ji**	11 o'clock	**jūichi-ji**
6 o'clock	**roku-ji**	12 o'clock	**jūni-ji**

Minutes

The minutes are shown below. To form 2 to 9 minutes, add -pun or -fun after the numbers. **Ip-pun**, *1 minute*, and **jup-pun**, *10 minutes*, have gone through phonetic changes. Notice that there are two forms each for *6 minutes* and *8 minutes*, and they are both used interchangeably.

1 minute	**ip-pun**	6 minutes	**rop-pun**
2 minutes	**ni-fun**	7 minutes	**nana-fun****
3 minutes	**san-pun**	8 minutes	**hachi-fun**
4 minutes	**yon-fun****	8 minutes	**hap-pun**
5 minutes	**go-fun**	9 minutes	**kyū-fun****
6 minutes	**roku-fun**	10 minutes	**jup-pun**

▶

*Note that **shi**, 4, **nana**, 7, and **kyū**, 9, are not used to indicate hours.
** Note that **shi**, 4, **nana**, 7, and **kyū**, 9, are not used to indicate minutes.

93

Minutes 10-60

When you put *jū*, *10*; *nijū*, *20*; *sanjū*, *30*; *yonjū*, *40* and
gojū, *50* before the minutes 1 to 9, you can form *11
minutes, 12 minutes, 59 minutes*. You obtain 20, 30, 40, 50
and 60 minutes by putting *ni*, *2*; *san*, *3*; *yon*, *4*; *go*, *5* and
roku, *6*, in front of *jup-pun*, *10 minutes*; this
forms *nijup-pun*, *sanjup-pun*, *yonjup-pun*, *gojup-pun* and
rokujup-pun respectively.

Putting 10 in front of 1, 2, 3 and 4 minutes, you get:

jū-ip-pun	11 minutes
jū-ni-fun	12 minutes
jū-san-pun	13 minutes
jū-yon-fun	14 minutes

Putting 20 in front of 1, 2, 3 and 4 minutes, you get:

nijū-ip-fun	21 minutes
nijū-ni-fun	22 minutes
nijū-san-pun	23 minutes
nijū-yon-fun	24 minutes

Putting 30, 40 and 50 in front of 1 minute, you get:

sanjū-ip-pun	31 minutes
yonjū-ip-pun	41 minutes
gojū-ip-pun	51 minutes

Putting 50 in front of 5 and 6 minutes, you get:

gojū-go-fun	55 minutes
gojū-roku-fun	56 minutes
gojū-rop-pun	56 minutes

How to Tell Time

In Japanese, you tell the time by saying the hour followed by the minute. It is written *hour:minute* just like it is in English.

2:15	*ni-ji jūgo-fun*
9:35	*ku-ji sanjūgo-fun*

Japanese has expressions such as *before/after* the hour just like English does. In these cases, **mae/sugi**, *before/after*, is put after the hour to indicate *before* or *after* as follows.

before 3 o'clock	*san-ji mae*
after 3 o'clock	*san-ji sugi*

Japanese has expressions such as *to/past* the hour just like English does. In these cases, **mae/sugi** is put after the minutes to indicate *to* or *past*.

5 minutes to 3 o'clock	*san-ji go-fun mae*
5 minutes past 3 o'clock	*san-ji go-fun sugi*

Although there is no special word for a quarter of an hour, Japanese has **han** for *half past,* which is put after the hour. 9:30 may be expressed in the following ways.

9:30	*ku-ji sanjup-pun*
30 minutes past 9 o'clock	*ku-ji sanjup-pun sugi*
half past 9	*ku-ji han*

Gozen and **gogo** are used for *a.m.* and *p.m.*, and they come before the hour.

2:15 p.m.	*gogo ni-ji jūgo-fun*
9:35 a.m.	*gozen ku-ji sanjūgo-fun*

Time Words

The suffixes and nouns associated with time are collected below.

han half past hour   **gogo** p.m.
mae before(hour)/(minutes)to   **gozen** a.m.
sugi after(hour)/(minute)past

-fun/pun is put after a number to tell minutes, and it is translated as *minutes*.
-ji is put after a number to tell the hour, and it is translated as *o'clock*.

Exercise 1

You will hear some times in Japanese. Write down each time in English.

1. _____

2. _____

3. _____

4. _____

5. _____

6. _____

Exercise 2

Say the following times aloud in Japanese, and check your answers on the CD.

1. 2:15
2. 4:30
3. 6:00
4. 8:40
5. 10:20
6. 12:00

How to Ask the Date and Time

The prefix **nan-**, *what*, is put before **nen**, **gatsu**, **nichi**, **yōbi**, **ji** and **fun** to obtain the following expressions.

nan-nen	What year?
nan-gatsu	What month?
nan-nichi	What date (of the month)?
nan-yōbi	What day of the week?
nan-ji	What time?/What hour?
nan-fun	How many minutes?

You can ask the date and time using the following words.

now	**ima**
today	**kyō**

What day (month and day) is it today?
Kyō wa nan-gatsu nan-nichi desu ka.

It's the 20th of March.
(Kyō wa) san-gatsu hatsuka desu.

What day of the week is the 3rd of March?
San-gatsu mikka wa nan-yōbi desu ka.

What time is it now?
Ima (wa) nan-ji desu ka.

It is 3 o'clock.
(Ima wa) san-ji desu.

Other Suffixes Associated with Numbers

One of the more difficult features of the Japanese number system is the concept of classifiers, special words that are attached after numbers to show categories of objects to which they belong. For instance, in English, you talk of *two* <u>sheets</u> *of paper* (rather than *two papers*), *three* <u>cups</u> *of water* (rather than *three waters*) or *two* <u>pieces</u> *of cake.* ▶

The words *sheet, cup* and *piece* are called classifiers because they classify the category of things, namely papers, liquid and slices.

In the Japanese number system, most things are described in terms of classifiers. The following vocabulary lists the classifiers associated with counting animals, just to illustrate a few of the many classifiers that exist in Japanese.

-hiki is put after a number to count animals such as dogs, tigers, rabbits*, fish and insects.

-tō is put after a number to count animals such as whales, cows and horses.

-nin is put after a number to count people.

-wa is put after a number to count animals such as rabbits*, and birds such as ducks and chickens.

Classifiers go through some phonetic changes when they are combined with some numbers (e.g., **ichi-hiki** becomes **ippiki**).

Here are two more important suffixes.

-ban is put after a number to tell the order. For example, **ichi-ban** means *number one*; **ni-ban** means *number two*; etc.

-mai is put after a number to count thin flat objects such as stamps, papers, tickets, plates, blankets, etc.

Numbers are not followed by any particle.

May I have three tickets please?   ***Kippu o san-mai kudasai.***
Mother buys two fish.   ***Okāsan wa sakana o ni-hiki kaimasu.***

*Note that rabbits are counted with both **-hiki** and **-wa**.

Translate the times into English:

1. jūichi-ji nijūgo-fun sugi _____

2. ku-ji jūnana-fun mae_____

3. gogo roku-ji sanjup-pun _____

4. go-ji han _____

Write the times in rōmaji and say them aloud:

5. 1:15 p.m. _____

6. 12:30 p.m. _____

7. 6:45 a.m. _____

8. 7:23 p.m. _____

Exercise 3

Choice of Japanese Speech Style

There are four levels of speech style in Japanese: polite, plain, honorific and rude.

Polite Speech

Polite speech is used in formal situations, such as when you speak in public, in business, while shopping, and to strangers or superiors. It is characterized by the use of the polite verbal forms *desu* and *V•masu*.

In this book, you will learn polite speech. It is safer to be polite than plain, and honorific speech is not called for on the part of a foreign speaker.

Plain Speech

Plain speech is used in informal, everyday situations among family, friends, equals, or when addressing children. For example, if you replace *desu* with *da* in a polite-style sentence, it will become a plain-style sentence: *kore wa inu da* is a plain form of *kore wa inu desu*, *this is a dog*.

▶

99

Similarly, by changing the endings of **V•masu**-verbs, you may convert polite-style **V•masu**-verb sentences into plain-style sentences. For example, **mizu o nomu** is a plain form of (**watashi wa**) **mizu o nomimasu**.

Honorific Speech

Use honorific speech to express respect. For example, a clerk in a shop would use honorific speech to a customer; if you were talking to your teacher or supervisor, you would use honorific speech. There are two ways to show your respect for others in honorofic speech.

<u>Method 1:</u> The most common form of expressing your respect is by using **o** or **go** as a prefix to nouns and adjectives when referring to the person or his belongings.

Kore wa boku no tegami desu.
This is my letter.
Kore wa sensei no (o)tegami desu.
This is the teacher's letter.

In some words, honorific prefixes have become so common that they have lost their honorific meaning and are thought of as a part of words. For instance, (**o**)**cha** is almost always used to mean *tea*: its plain form **cha** is rarely used. Not every noun or adjective takes an honorific prefix and there is no specific rule as to whether a word is prefixed by **o** or **go**. You should not try to make honorific words up by yourself until you have reached a more advanced level of proficiency in the language.

Another common way of expressing your respect is to add **-san** to a person's family, as shown below.

Kore wa anata no imōto-san desu ka.
Is this your younger sister?
Hai kore wa watashi no imōto desu.
Yes, this is my younger sister.

▶

<u>Method 2:</u> You may show your respect by using humble terms for yourself and your belongings.

Expressing deeper respect for the other person creates a greater distance between you both, and, unless you are advanced in Japanese, you should not try to use honorific speech.

Rude Speech

Rude speech may be used toward inferiors, or in insults, and you should obviously avoid it.

Practice the five hiragana characters *ma, mi, mu, me* and *mo.*

 and **も.**

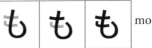

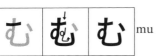

I Do That, Too!

Dialogue 1

Hanako: Anata mo* kōhī o nomimasen ka.
Tom: Hai (boku mo kōhī o) nomimasu.
Hanako: Anata no otōsan to okāsan wa Nihon-go o
hanashimasu ka.
Tom: Hai (Boku no) otōsan mo okāsan mo (Nihon-
go o) hanashimasu. (Boku no) otōsan wa
Furansu-go mo hanashimasu.
Hanako: Watashi no onēsan mo Furansu-go o hanashi-
masu.

***Anata mo** is put in the sentence to emphasize that the
meaning is *you too.*

My Father Speaks French, Too

Hanako asks Tom about his parents' skill in Japanese.

Hanako: Would you also like to drink coffee?
Tom: Yes, I would.
Hanako: Do your father and mother speak Japanese?
Tom: Yes, both (my) father and (my) mother speak
Japanese.
My father speaks French too.
Hanako: My older sister also speaks French.

The Particle Mo

The particle **mo** means *also/too*. **Mo** is placed after the word to which it refers. If **mo** refers to a subject, it replaces the particle **wa** or **ga** (discussed later). If **mo** refers to a direct object, it replaces **o**. However, if the noun **mo** refers/to/a word that is followed by the particle **de** or **ni/e** (discussed in a later lesson), the particle remains, and **mo** comes after the particle.

I read a book.	**Watashi wa hon o yomimasu.**
Father also reads a book.	**Otōsan mo hon o yomimasu.**
Father reads a book.	**Otōsan wa hon o yomimasu.**
Father reads a magazine also (as well as a book).	**Otōsan wa zasshi mo yomimasu.**
This is a book.	**Kore wa hon desu.**
That also is a book.	**Are mo hon desu.**
I read a book in my room.	**Watashi wa hon o watashi no heya de yomimasu.**
I read a book in the living room also	**Watashi wa hon o ima de mo yomimasu.**

If each noun in a list is followed by **mo**, this means *both _ and _*.

Both younger sister and older sister read books.	**Imōto mo onēsan mo hon o yomimasu.**
The cat eats both fish and meat.	**Neko wa sakana mo niku mo tabemasu.**

For negative verbs, _ **mo** _ **mo** means *neither _ nor _*.

Neither the younger sister nor the older sister reads books.	**Imōto mo onēsan mo hon o yomimasen.**
A rabbit eats neither fish nor meat.	**Usagi wa sakana mo niku mo tabemasen.**

Exercise 1

Combine the two sentences into one sentence.

1. Watashi wa tegami o kōkūbin de okurimasu. Imōto mo tegami o kōkūbin de okurimasu.

Watashi _____ imōto _____ tegami o kōkūbin de okurimasu.

Both my sister and I send letters by airmail.

2. Ashita watashi wa ban-gohan o ie de tabemasen. Ashita otōto mo ban-gohan o ie de tabemasen.

Ashita watashi _____ otōto _____ ban-gohan o ie de tabemasen.

Neither my younger brother nor I will eat dinner at home tomorrow.

The Particle Ni after Specific Time

Time expressions may be separated into three different categories: "specific time", "general time" and "relative time".

"Specific time" is time that may be indicated as a point on a calendar or clock (1 o'clock, March 25). "Relative time" is time that depends on when "now" is, such as *last month, next year* and *tomorrow.* "General time" is time in general such as *everyday, morning* and *spring.*

When you use time expressions, the time expression is put at the beginning of a sentence or just after the subject (and its particle). The time expression must be followed by *ni, at/in/on,* if it indicates "specific time."

At 8 o'clock, I watch TV.
Hachi-ji ni watashi wa terebi o mimasu.
I watch TV at 8 o'clock.
Watashi wa hachi-ji ni terebi o mimasu.

In September, we shall learn Japanese.
Ku-gatsu ni watashi-tachi wa Nihon-go o naraimasu.
I drink coffee at 9 o'clock also (as well as at 8 o'clock).
Ku-ji ni mo watashi wa kōhī o nomimasu.

Seasons: Time in General

When discussing general time, you do not put any particle after the time expression.

The following is a list of words that are used to refer to general time.

morning	*asa*	spring	*haru*
afternoon	*hiru*	summer	*natsu*
evening	*ban*	autumn	*aki*
night	*yoru*	winter	*fuyu*

In summer, we will learn English.
Natsu watashi-tachi wa Eigo o naraimasu.

We will learn English in summer.
Watashi-tachi wa natsu Eigo o naraimasu.

Do you watch TV at night?
Yoru anata wa terebi o mimasu ka.

Write **ni** in the blanks wherever it is needed, and then translate the sentences into English.

1. Asa no hachi-ji _____ watashi-tachi wa asa-gohan

   o tabemasu.

   We eat breakfast at 8 o'clock in the morning.

2. Roku-ji _____ otōsan wa ban-gohan o tabemasen.

   _____

3. Yoru _____ watashi-tachi wa terebi o mimasu.

   _____

4. Natsu _____ otōsan wa ie o urimasu.

   _____

Exercise 2

The Particle Ni after an Indirect Object

There are two types of action verbs: transitive verbs and intransitive verbs. A transitive verb may have a direct object and an indirect object. A direct object is the person/thing/ matter to which the verb directs its action. An indirect object is the person/thing for whom the action is taking place. In most cases, the words *to* or *for* can be inserted before the indirect object. Consider the following two sentences.

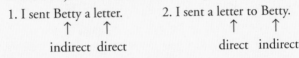

1. I sent Betty a letter.   2. I sent a letter to Betty.
      ↑   ↑   ↑   ↑
   indirect direct   direct   indirect

The sentences 1 and 2 have the same meaning, but in different forms. *Letter* is what was *sent* and therefore it is the direct object; *Betty* is the person to whom the letter is sent and therefore it is the indirect object.

An indirect object, which may be preceeded by *to* or *for* in English, must be followed by **ni** in Japanese.

Addressing Letters and Post Cards

In Japan, *hagaki* (plain post cards) are very widely used. You write the addresses and names of both the sender and the receiver on the front of the post card: larger characters are used for the receiver and smaller characters for the sender. All messages are written on the back of the post card. Special post cards are issued every year for the New Year celebration and Summer Season greetings.

On an envelope, the address and the name of the receiver are written in front while the sender's address and name are written on the back with smaller characters.

Japanese post offices are marked with 〒. They have banking services and insurance services, as well as the usual postal services. You must go to the counter marked はがき・切手 for stamps, post cards and the other usual postal services.

Dialogue 2

Hanako:	Nan-ji ni (anata wa) asa-gohan o tabemasu ka.
Tom:	Asa no shichi-ji han ni (boku wa asa-gohan o) tabemasu.
Hanako:	(Anata wa) nani o (asa-gohan ni) tabemasu ka.
Tom:	(Boku wa asa-gohan ni) pan o tabemasu. (Boku wa) kōhī mo nomimasu.
Hanako:	Nan-ji ni (anata wa) ban-gohan o tabemasu ka.
Tom:	Roku-ji ni (boku-tachi wa ban-gohan o) tabemasu.
Hanako:	Yoru (anata wa) hon o yomimasu ka.
Tom:	Hai yomimasu. (Yoru boku wa) terebi mo mimasu.

asa-gohan	breakfast
ban-gohan	dinner
ranchi	lunch
hiru-gohan	lunch
gohan	meal, boiled rice

What Time Do You Eat Breakfast?

Hanako asks Tom about his daily eating habits.

Hanako:	What time do you eat (your) breakfast?
Tom:	I eat at 7:30 in the morning.
Hanako:	What do you eat?
Tom:	I eat bread. I drink coffee too.
Hanako:	What time do you eat (your) dinner?
Tom:	We eat at 6 o'clock.
Hanako:	Do you read books at night?
Tom:	Yes, I do. I watch TV too.

Exercise 3

You will hear some questions about Dialogue 2. Reply to each question aloud in Japanese. Write your answers below, and check them on the CD.

1. _____

2. _____

3. _____

4. _____

Exercise 4

Translate into English:

1. Watashi wa mizu o nomimasu. _____

Imōto mo mizu o nomimasu. _____

2. Okāsan mo otōsan mo hon o heya de yomimasu.

_____

3. Ashita anata mo watashi-tachi to bideo o mimasen ka.

_____

4. Yoru watashi-tachi wa tegami o tomodachi ni kakimasu.

_____

5. Ichi-ji ni Igirisu-jin wa ranchi o tabemasu. _____

_____

Translate into rōmaji:

6. Hanako does not read French books. _____

_____

Makoto also does not read French books. _____

_____

7. In December, we send presents to (our) grandfather and grandmother. _____

_____

▶

8. I speak both English and Japanese. _____

_____

9. Neither (my) father nor (my) mother speaks English.

_____

10. At twelve o'clock, we listen to Japanese music on the radio.

_____

_____

🔊 More Transitive Verbs

Here are some more verbs that you can use in the
sentence structure _ **wa** _ **o V•masu.**

collect	**atsumemasu**	resign from, quit	**yamemasu**
choose	**erabimasu**		
return (things borrowed)	**kaeshimasu**	give (to somebody)	**agemasu**
borrow	**karimasu**	give (to me)	**kuremasu**
lend	**kashimasu**	put on (footwear, trousers)	**hakimasu**
wait for	**machimasu**		
invite	**manekimasu**	put on (hat)	**kaburimasu**
show	**misemasu**		
lose	**nakushimasu**	put on (dress)	**kimasu**
stop(vehicles)	**tomemasu**		
forget	**wasuremasu**		

I stop (my) car here.
Boku wa kuruma o koko de tomemasu.

I give you this. (I give this to you.)
Watashi wa kore o anata ni agemasu.

Will you give me this?
Anata wa kore o watashi ni kuremasu ka.

Tomorrow, I will return you this. (return this to you.)
Ashita watashi wa kore o anata ni kaeshimasu.

▶

From 9 o'clock, they will show an Italian movie on TV.
Ku-ji kara Itaria no eiga o terebi de misemasu.

In September, the history teacher resigns from the school.
Ku-gatsu ni rekishi no sensei wa gakkō o yamemasu.

At 8 o'clock, I'll wait for you at the station.
Hachi-ji ni watashi wa anata o eki de machimasu.

The verb *wait* is followed by *for* in English. The Japanese equivalent **machimasu** is a transitive verb and is preceded by **o**. Similarly, the verb *resign* is followed by *from* in English. The Japanese equivalent **yamemasu** is a transitive verb and is also preceded by **o**.

 To Put On

There are three different words for *put on* (clothing) in Japanese. Use **kaburimasu** for put on <u>on the head</u>, **kimasu** for put on <u>above the waist and below the head</u>, and **hakimasu** for put on <u>below the waist</u>. The following vocabulary lists some clothing that you may put on your body.

hat	**bōshi**	shoe	**kutsu**
blouse	**burausu**	sock, stocking	**kutsushita**
dress	**doresu**	sweater	**sētā**
clothes, clothing	**fuku**	skirt	**sukāto**
		suit	**sūtsu**
kimono	**kimono**	one-piece dress	**wanpīsu**
coat	**kōto**	trousers, pants	**zubon**

Exercise 5

⊙ You will hear the narrator talk about things she does. Respond to each phrase by saying that you do that thing too. Check your replies against the correct answers on the CD.

1. _____

2. _____

3. _____

4. _____

Exercise 6

Translate into English:

1. Watashi wa kore o karimasu. _____
_____

2. Haru sensei wa gakkō o yamemasu. _____
_____

3. Natsu okāsan wa obāsan o Nihon ni manekimasu. _____
_____

4. Otōsan wa kuruma o doko de tomemasu ka. _____
_____

5. Anata wa fuyu bōshi o kaburimasu ka. _____
_____

Translate into rōmaji:

6. My younger brother and I invite Robert to our house.

_____

▶

7. My older sister collects hats. _____
_____

8. I will not forget you. _____
_____

9. In winter, do you put on a coat?_____
_____

10. I will not show (my) painting to (my) father. _____
_____

Practice the three hiragana characters *ya, yu* and *yo*.

や,　ゆ　and　よ.

Writing Exercise

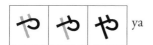
ya

yu

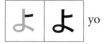
yo

Would You Like To...?

🔊 Dialogue 1

Tom:	Moshi-moshi.
Hanako:	Moshi-moshi. (Anata wa) Tom-kun desu ka.
Tom:	Hai (boku wa Tom desu). Hanako-san Konban-wa.
Hanako:	Konbanwa. San-gatsu nijūichi-nichi no hiru (ni) anata wa hima desu ka.
Tom:	(San-gatsu nijūichi-nichi wa) nan-yōbi desu ka.
Hanako:	(San-gatsu nijūichi-nichi wa) do-yōbi desu.
Tom:	(Boku wa) hima desu.
Hanako:	San-gatsu nijūichi-nichi wa watashi no bāsudē desu. Bāsudē pātī* ni kimasen ka.
Tom:	Hai (Boku wa bāsudē pātī ni) ikimasu. (Bāsudē pātī wa) nan-ji kara nan-ji made desu ka.
Hanako:	(Bāsudē pātī wa) jūni-ji kara yo-ji made desu.

bāsudē	birthday
hima	free, time to spare
pātī	party

*Lately, many foreign words (mostly English words) have become Japanese. In order to make the sounds as close as possible to the original English sounds, new syllables such as *ti* are introduced into Japanese.

▶

Would You Like to Come to My Birthday Party?

Hanako calls Tom to invite him to her birthday party.

Tom:	Hello!
Hanako:	Hello! Is that (Are you) Tom?
Tom:	Yes. Good evening Hanako.
Hanako:	Good evening.
	Are you free in the afternoon of March 21st?
Tom:	What day of the week is it?
Hanako:	It's a Saturday.
Tom:	I'm free.
Hanako:	March 21st is my birthday.
	Would you like to come to (my) birthday party?
Tom:	Yes, I would.
	From what time to what time is it?
Hanako:	It's from 12 o'clock to 4 o'clock.

💿 Dialogue 2

Tom: Hanako-san Konnichiwa.
Hanako: Tom-kun Konnichiwa. (O)genki desu ka.
Tom: Hai genki desu. (O)genki desu ka.
Hanako: Hai okagesama de. (Anata wa) doko e ikimasu ka.
Tom: (Boku wa) yūbinkyoku e ikimasu.
            (Boku wa) tegami o ojīsan ni okurimasu.
Hanako: (Anata wa) tegami o Nihon-go de ojīsan ni
            kakimasu ka.
Tom: Iie (boku wa tegami o) Eigo de kakimasu.
            Ojīsan wa Nihon-go o yomimasen.
            Haru ojīsan wa Nihon e kimasu.
Hanako: (Ojīsan wa Nihon e) hikōki de kimasu ka.
Tom: Hai (ojīsan wa Nihon e hikōki de kimasu).
Hanako: Ojīsan wa Nihon-go o hanashimasu ka.
Tom: Iie hanashimasen.
Hanako: Watashi wa Eigo o naraimasu.
            (Watashi wa) Eigo o ojīsan ni hanashimasu.
            Dewa mata. Sayōnara.
Tom: Sayōnara.

Is He Coming by Airplane?

Tom meets Hanako on his way to a post office.

Tom: Good afternoon, Hanako.
Hanako: Good afternoon, Tom. How are you?
Tom: I am fine. How are you?
Hanako: I am fine, thank you. Where are you going?
Tom: I am going to the post office.
            I am sending a letter to (my) grandfather.
Hanako: Do you write letters to (your) grandfather in
            Japanese?

Tom:	No, I write in English.
	(My) grandfather does not read Japanese.
	In spring, (my) grandfather is coming to Japan.
Hanako:	Is he coming by airplane?
Tom:	Yes.
Hanako:	Does (your) grandfather speak Japanese?
Tom:	No, he doesn't.
Hanako:	I'll learn English.
	I'll speak English to (your) grandfather.
	See you. Good-bye.
Tom:	Good-bye.

🔵 *Verbs of Motion*

go out	*demasu*	return	*kaerimasu*
come in, join,	*hairimasu*	come	*kimasu*
get in		get off	*orimasu*
go	*ikimasu*		

Verbs of motion have the sentence structure

<u>subject</u> *wa* <u>place</u> *e/kara V•masu*.

The particle *wa* follows the subject, the particle *e/kara*
follows the place of motion *to/from*. The verb of motion
V•masu is placed at the end of the sentence.

Note that *e* is translated as *to* in the sense of motion towards
a place. It should not be confused with giving *to* which
requires *ni*, as you learned in the previous lesson.

Places

Here are some words you can use when talking about places you go.

primary school	**shōgakkō**	company	**kaisha**
secondary school	**chūgakkō**	factory	**kōjō**
		meeting	**kaigi**
cram school	**juku**	work	**shigoto**
high school	**kōkō**	lecture	**jugyō**
technical college	**kōgyō-daigaku**	(lecture) class	**kurasu**
		coffee shop	**kissaten**
university	**daigaku**	bath	**furo**

Here are some typical sentences using verbs of motion.

I go to America with (my) father.
Watashi wa Amerika e otōsan to ikimasu.

Father will come here.
Otōsan wa koko e kimasu.

Father returns from work (company).
Otōsan wa kaisha kara kaerimasu.

Grandmother gets off (from) the bus.
Obāsan wa basu kara orimasu.

 Transportation

You can make sentences more complete by saying when, and how, you go somewhere.

ship, boat	**fune**	car	**kuruma**
airplane	**hikōki**	motorcycle	**ōtobai**
automobile	**jidōsha**	scooter	**sukūtā**
bicycle	**jitensha**	taxi	**takushī**
train	**kisha**	truck	**torakku**

In summer, we go to school by bicycle.
Natsu watashi-tachi wa gakkō e jitensha de ikimasu.

In August, Tom will return from America by airplane.
Hachi-gatsu ni Tom-kun wa Amerika kara hikōki de kaerimasu.

(My) father will come here by (his) car at 9 o'clock.
Ku-ji ni otōsan wa koko e kuruma de kimasu.

Asking Someone Out for Lunch

When you are going to an event, and not to a place, ***ni*** follows the event and is translated as *to*. An event should never be followed by ***e***. Using this construction, you can ask someone to go somewhere with you, as in the examples below.

Would you like to come to dinner?
Ban-gohan ni kimasen ka.

I will go to a Japanese lecture.
Watashi wa Nihon-go no jugyō ni ikimasu.

Would you like to go to a movie on Saturday?
Do-yōbi ni eiga ni ikimasen ka.

Ni and Kara

Instead of saying *take a bath* and *finish a bath*, Japanese uses ***furo ni hairimasu***, *come into a bath*, and ***furo kara demasu***, *go out from a bath*, since Japanese bathing involves getting into and out of a bathtub.

I take a bath at night.   ***Watashi wa yoru furo ni hairimasu.***

Father finishes (his) bath.   ***Otosan wa furo kara demasu.***

When you are making an arrangement for a party or a meeting, you'll want to tell the other person when the event will start and end. In this case, you use the expression **A kara B made**, implying *from A to B*. **A kara B made** can also denote locations.

from 9 o'clock till 10 o'clock   ***ku-ji kara ju-ji made***
from Osaka to Tokyo   ***Ōsaka kara Tōkyō made***

Moshi-moshi

When you talk to a person on the telephone, you always say **moshi-moshi** for *hello*. The person on the other line will also reply **moshi-moshi**, *hello*. **Moshi-moshi** is used only on the telephone.

Exercise 1

Your friend is inviting you to various activities. Listen to the phrases on the CD, and write the activities in English.

1. _____

2. _____

3. _____

4. _____

5. _____

6. _____

Exercise 2

🔘 Listen to the phrases on the CD and answer the questions in rōmaji.

1. Otōsan wa doko e kisha de ikimasu ka. _____

_____

2. Okāsan wa sūpāmāketto e nan de ikimasu ka._____

_____

3. Imōto wa gakkō e basu de ikimasu ka. _____

_____

4. Onēsan wa doko e ikimasu ka. _____

_____

Exercise 3

Make sentences by matching each phrase on the left with the correct phrase on the right.

1. Ichi-gatsu kara go-gatsu made • watashi wa kisha de ikimasu.

2. Tōkyō kara Ōsaka made • otōto wa terebi o mimasu.

3. Asa kara yoru made • otōsan wa gaikoku e ikimasu.

Now translate the complete sentences into English.

1. _____

2. _____

3. _____

Translate into English.

1. Ichi-gatsu ni Betty-san wa Amerika e kaerimasu. _____
_____

2. Anata wa doko e kisha de ikimasu ka. _____
_____

3. Onēsan mo basu kara orimasu._____

4. Otōto mo watashi mo gakkō e kuruma de ikimasen. _____
_____

5. Haru ojīsan wa Nihon e fune de kimasu. _____
_____

Translate into rōmaji:

6. Father comes out of (goes out from) a bath.
_____

7. I go to school at 8 o'clock in the morning.
_____

8. In September, I shall go to America by airplane._____
_____

9. Tom will not go back (return) to America in summer. _____
_____

10. My younger brother does not enter kindergarten in
September. _____
_____

The Japanese Hostess

When you are invited to a Japanese home, you may notice that the lady of the house rarely joins you in the conversation, especially if you are a guest of the man of the house. Instead, she stays in the kitchen preparing dishes to serve. It is usual for only the man of the house to eat with the guest.

Practice the five hiragana characters **ra, ri, ru, re** and **ro.**

ら， り， る， れ and ろ.

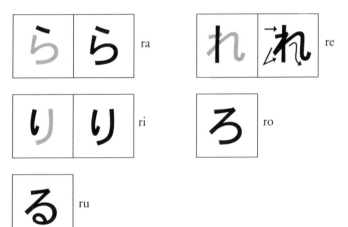

ra

re

ri

ro

ru

What Do You Do?

 Dialogue 1

Hanako:	Raishū wa Gōruden-uīku desu. Daigaku wa yasumi desu.
Tom:	(Yasumi wa) itsu kara itsu made desu ka.
Hanako:	(Yasumi wa) getsu-yōbi kara kin-yōbi made desu.
Tom:	Raishū (anata wa) nani o shimasu ka.
Hanako:	(Watashi-tachi wa) ryokō o shimasu. (Watashi-tachi wa) ojīsan to obāsan no ie e iki masu.
Tom:	(Anata wa) nani o ojīsan to obāsan no ie de shmasu ka.
Hanako:	Okāsan to obāsan wa ryōri o shimasu. Watashi wa tetsudai o shimasu.
Tom:	Anata wa benkyō o shimasu ka.
Hanako:	Iie shimasen.

Gōruden-uīku	Golden-Week
yasumi	holiday
itsu	when

What are you doing next week?

Hanako tells Tom about the Golden-Week holiday.

Hanako:	Next week is Golden-Week. Colleges are on holiday.
Tom:	From when to when is it?
Hanako:	From Monday to Friday.
Tom:	What are you doing next week?

▶

Hanako:	We are going to travel.
	We are going to (our) grandfather and grandmother's house.
Tom:	What do you do at (your) grandfather and grandmother's house?
Hanako:	(My) mother and (my) grandmother cook. I help (them).
Tom:	Do you study?
Hanako:	No, I don't.

Shimasu

<u>subject</u> **wa** <u>direct object</u> **o shimasu**

Shimasu, *do*, is a very useful transitive verb; it has the sentence structure _ **wa** _ **o shimasu**, just like other transitive verbs. With this verb, you can find out more about someone, or talk more about yourself, by forming sentences like, *Do you cook?*, *Do you play tennis?* or *I study Japanese.*

What Do You Do?

These nouns may be used with **shimasu** as direct objects, to describe what you, or others, do.

greeting	**aisatsu**	cooking	**ryōri**
knitting	**amimono**	laundry	**sentaku**
study	**benkyō**	cleaning	**sōji**
date	**deito**	help	**tetsudai**
conversation	**hanashi**	driving	**unten**
shopping	**kaimono**	promise	**yakusoku**
marriage	**kekkon**	travel	**ryokō**

I Cook, I Study: Nouns with O Shimasu

Unlike the English language where the verb *do* emphasizes actions (e.g., I *do* greet, I *do* study, etc.), there is no such emphasis with **shimasu**. **Shimasu** just converts some nouns into single verbs. Hence, "noun + **o** + **shimasu**" may be translated as a single verb as follows.

aisatsu o shimasu	means *greet* rather than *do greet*.
benkyō o shimasu	means *study* rather than *do study*.
amimono o shimasu	means *knit* rather than *do knit*.

Okāsan wa amimono o shimasu.	Mother knits.
Otōsan wa ryokō o shimasu.	Father travels.
Anata wa nani o shimasu ka.	What do you do?
Ryōri o shimasen ka.	Would you like to cook?
Otōsan wa aisatsu o sensei ni* shimasu.	The father greets the teacher.

When the direct objects are sports, such as those listed below, **shimasu** may be translated as *do, play, practice*, etc., according to context.

sports	**supōtsu**	sumo wrestling	**sumō**
judo	**jūdō**	gymnastics	**taisō**
karate	**karate**	tennis	**tenisu**
swimming	**suiei**	baseball	**yakyū**

practice karate	**karate o shimasu**
play tennis	**tenisu o shimasu**
swim	**suiei o shimasu**
do not play baseball	**yakyū o shimasen**

* Note that **sensei** is an indirect object in the Japanese sentence, so it is followed by **ni**.

Being More Specific: Noun + No + O Shimasu

Some nouns may be expanded with **no** and used with **shimasu** as shown below.

ryōri	cooking
sakana no ryōri	cooking of fish
sakana no ryōri o shimasu	(I) cook fish
hanashi	talk
Kanada no hanashi	talk about Canada
Kanada no hanashi o shimasu	(I) talk about Canada
Watashi wa Nihon-go no benkyō o shimasu.	I study Japanese.
Anata wa nan no supōtsu o shimasu ka.	What sports do you do?

Holidays

A working person usually has three one-week holidays per year. They are New Year's Holiday (around New Year's Day), "Golden-Week" (a string of national holidays from April 29 to May 5) and **O-Bon** (around August 13–August 16).

O-Bon is a Buddhist festival to commemorate deceased family members. According to Japanese tradition, spirits of the deceased wander in space not far from home, usually for thirty-three years, after the bodies die; they return once a year for a short visit, arriving on the evening of August 13 and returning to the spirit world on August 16.

Exercise 1

You will hear some things that Hanako's older sister does on Saturdays. Answer the questions in rōmaji.

1. Asa hachi-ji ni onēsan wa nani o shimasu ka._____

_____

2. Asa onēsan wa sentaku to sōji o shimasu ka. _____

_____

3. Hiru onēsan wa nani o shimasu ka. _____

_____

4. Ban onēsan wa nani o shimasu ka. _____

_____

Exercise 2

Translate into English:

1. ryokō o shimasu_____

2. sumō o shimasen _____

3. Yoru okāsan wa amimono mo shimasu._____

_____

4. Onīsan wa yakyū o shimasen. _____

_____

Translate into rōmaji:

5. promise _____

6. do not play tennis _____

7. In August, we travel by car._____

8. What do you do at school? _____

| **Sumō** | ***Sumō*** wrestling is one of the most popular spectator sports in Japan. Two huge men, wearing only loin cloths, push |

each other in a small ring covered with sand. The rule for winning is very simple. One has to push the opponent out of the ring, or, get any part of his body, except the soles of the feet, to touch the ground.

Verbs: Noun + Shimasu

Some of the nouns that you have learned may be combined directly with **shimasu** to form single verbs.

ryokō shimasu	to travel
kekkon shimasu	to marry
unten shimasu	to drive
benkyō shimasu	to study
ryōri shimasu	to cook
sentaku shimasu	to do laundry
sōji shimasu	to clean
yakusoku shimasu	to promise

The above nouns + **shimasu** can also be made more specific with the sentence structure

<u>subject</u> **wa** <u>direct object</u> **o** <u>noun</u> **+ shimasu**

Watashi wa Nihon-go o benkyo shimasu.
I study Japanese

Watashi wa seta o sentaku shimasu.
I wash (my) sweater.

Watashi-tachi wa Kyōto o ryokō shimasu.
We travel in Kyoto.

Although *to travel* does not take a direct object in English, **ryōko shimasu** follows **o** and should be translated according to context.

To date, To marry

Although *to date* and *to marry* may be transitive verbs in English (we may say *I date Betty* and *I marry Betty* in English), the equivalent **deito shimasu**, *to date*, and **kekkon shimasu**, *to marry*, are not transitive verbs in Japanese. You must use expressions equivalent to *I date <u>with</u> Betty* and *I marry <u>with</u> Betty* in Japanese. Hence, **deito shimasu** and **kekkon shimasu** must follow the particle **to**, *together/along with* (and not **o**).

Watashi wa Betty-san to deito shimasu.
I date Betty.

Giving More Information

The sentence structure _ **wa** _ **o** "noun + **shimasu**" gives more information than the sentence structure _ **wa** _ **o shimasu** as can be seen from the examples below.

Watashi wa unten o shimasu.	I drive.
Watashi wa kuruma o unten shimasu.	I drive a car.
Watashi wa ryokō o shimasu.	I travel.
Watashi wa Nihon o ryokō shimasu.	I travel in Japan.

The following sentences have the same meaning. In the examples below, **Nihon-go no benkyō**, *study of Japanese*, and **sētā no sentaku**, *laundry of the sweater*, are treated as nouns.

Watashi wa Nihon-go o benkyō shimasu.	I study Japanese
Watashi wa Nihon-go no benkyō o shimasu.	I study Japanese.
Watashi wa sētā o sentaku shimasu.	I wash (my) sweater.
Watashi wa sētā no sentaku o shimasu.	I wash (my) sweater.

Rewrite the sentences with "noun + **o** + **shimasu**" to become sentences with "noun + **shimasu**."

1. Watashi wa niwa no sōji o shimasu.
   Watashi wa niwa o sōji shimasu.
2. Ojisan wa torakku no unten o shimasu.
   Ojisan wa_____
3. Okāsan wa yasai no ryōri o shimasu.
   Okāsan wa _____
4. Onēsan wa Eigo no benkyō o shimasu.
   Onēsan wa _____

Exercise 3

Translate into English:

1. Watashi wa kore o ryōri shimasu. _____
_____
2. Watashi wa sore o yakusoku shimasu._____
_____
3. Betty-san wa kuruma o unten shimasen. _____
_____
4. Hachi-gatsu ni watashi-tachi wa kekkon shimasu. _____
_____

Translate into rōmaji:

5. In fall, I shall travel in America. _____
_____
6. I cook steak for lunch._____
_____
7. In spring, I clean the garden. _____
_____
8. Does Tom study Japanese? _____
_____

Exercise 4

Could You Do Me a Favor? *Onegai shimasu*

When **shimasu** is combined with **onegai**, *appeal/wish*, it can mean many things. **Onegai shimasu**, which literally means *do wish* or *do appeal*, is a very useful expression to attract someone's attention and ask a favor; it means *I beg you* or *Please do this*.

Onegai shimasu is used in the following situations:

1. When calling a clerk in a store or a waiter in a restarant for service.

   Onegai shimasu.   Excuse me.

2. Ordering food in a restaurant.

   Sutēki onegai shimasu.   Steak, please.

3. When you don't understand the amount the salesperson said, you can ask the person to write it down, by handing over a pencil and paper and saying:

   Onegai shimasu.   Please (write it down).

4. When submitting bills or papers at a bank, a post office or a hospital.

   Onegai shimasu.   Please look after this.

5. When you wish to tell the elevator operator your floor.

   Go-kai onegai shimasu.   Fifth floor please.

6. When telling a taxi driver your destination.

   Eki onegai shimasu.   To the train station, please.

7. When you ask for somebody.

   Betty-san onegai shimasu.   May I speak to Betty please?

Note that the phrases are used in one-to-one conversations, and the direct objects of the verb **onegai shimasu** (**go-kai**, **eki**, etc.) are not followed by **o**.

Dialogue 2

Tom: (Boku-tachi wa) resutoran wa doko ni shimasu ka.
Hanako: (Watashi-tachi wa resutoran wa) Edo ni
            shimasen ka.
***

Tom: (Anata wa) tabemono wa nani ni shimasu ka.
Hanako: (Watashi wa tabemono wa) yakisoba ni shimasu.
            Anata wa (tabemono wa nani ni shimasu ka).
Tom: Boku wa (tabemono wa) tonkatsu ni shimasu.
            (Anata wa) nomimono wa (nani ni shimasu ka).
Hanako: (Watashi wa nomimono wa) miruku ni shimasu.
            Anata wa (nomimono wa nani ni shimasu ka).
Tom: Boku wa (nomimono wa) orenji-jūsu ni shimasu.

Which Restaurant Should We Got To?

Tom and Hanako go to a restaurant.

Tom: To which restaurant do we go? (Where do we
            decide on for a restaurant?)
Hanako: Would you like to go to Edo? (Would you like to
            decide on Edo?)

Tom and Hanako arrive at Edo restaurant.

Tom: What will you have for food?
Hanako: I'll have yakisoba.
            How about you?
Tom: I'll have a pork cutlet.
            How about the drinks?
Hanako: I'll have milk.
            How about you?
Tom: I'll have orange juice.

I Choose: Ni Shimasu

If you want to say that one *decides* or *chooses* something, you use the sentence structure

<u>what is chosen</u> **ni shimasu**, meaning *decide on _*.

This is an abbreviation of the sentence structure

<u>subject</u> **wa** <u>topic</u> **wa** <u>what is chosen</u> **ni shimasu.**

The first **wa** follows the person making the choice, the second **wa** follows the topic under discussion and is translated as *as for* or *for*, and **ni** follows what is chosen.

With this sentence structure, you can talk about very important decisions, like what to eat.

tabemono	food
Sushi ni shimasu.	Decide on sushi.
Are ni shimasu.	Decide on that.

Watashi wa tabemono wa sushi ni shimasu.
I shall have sushi. (I decide on sushi for food.)
Anata wa tabemono wa nani ni shimasu ka.
What will you eat? (What do you decide on for food?)

Exercise 5

Join each question on the left with a correct reply on the right.

Dore ni shimasu ka.   •   •   Koko ni shimasu.

Doko ni shimasu ka.   •   •   Kore ni shimasu.

Nan ni shimasu ka.   •

Translate into English using the context provided:

1. Byōin onegai shimasu. (in a taxi) _____

_____

2. Tom-kun onegai shimasu. (on a telephone)_____

_____

3. (Watashi-tachi wa) kudamono wa nani ni shimasu ka. _____

_____

4. Doko no (o)tera ni shimasu ka._____

_____

5. Dare no ie ni shimasu ka. _____

Translate into rōmaji:

6. Could you take me to the Tokyo zoo please? _____

_____

7. May I speak to the English teacher please?_____

_____

8. What do we decide on for a present for Hanako? _____

_____

9. On whom do we decide?_____

_____

10. Where do we decide on for travelling?_____

_____

Exercise 7

💿 You will hear some questions about Dialogue 2. Reply to each question aloud in Japanese, and check your answers on the CD.

Writing Exercise

Practice the three hiragana characters *wa, wo* and *n*.

わ、 を and ん.

| わ | わ | wa |

| を | を | を | wo |

| ん | n |

Martial Arts

In order to defend themselves against samurai, farmers and tradesmen developed many martial arts such as *karate* and *jūdō*. Deprived of owning weapons, they used simple sticks, mental preparedness and their bodies.

The Apple is Delicious

🔵 Dialogue 1

Hanako:	(Sore wa) kawaii inu desu ne.
	(Sore wa) anata no inu desu ka.
Tom:	Hai sō desu.
Hanako:	(Inu no) ashi wa mijikai desu ne.
Tom:	Kono inu wa dakkusufundo desu yo.
	Dakkusufundo no ashi wa mijikai desu yo.
Hanako:	(Inu no) me wa ōkii desu ne. (Inu no) mimi wa
	nagai desu ne. (Inu no) namae wa nan desu ka.
Tom:	(Inu no namae wa) Cute desu.
Hanako:	(Inu no namae wa) kawaii namae desu ne.
Tom:	CUTE wa Nihon-go de KAWAII desu.
Hanako:	(Cute wa) kono inu ni pittari na namae desu ne.

dakkusufundo	dachshund
pittari na	perfectly fit

He's a Cute Dog, Isn't he?

Hanako meets Tom, walking his dog.

Hanako:	He is a cute dog, isn't he? Is he your dog?
Tom:	Yes, he is.
Hanako:	The legs are short, aren't they?
Tom:	He (This dog) is a dachshund!
	A dachshund's legs are short!
Hanako:	His eyes are big, aren't they? His ears are long,
	aren't they? What is his name?
Tom:	It's Cute.
Hanako:	It's a cute name, isn't it?
Tom:	CUTE is KAWAII in Japanese.
Hanako:	It's a perfectly fit name, isn't it?

I-Adjectives

Look at the sampling of Japanese adjectives below.
Notice that the adjectives listed below end with _i_;
these adjectives are called *i*-adjectives for that reason.

warm	**atatakai**	cool	**suzushii**
hot (temperature)	**atsui**	cold (temperature)	**samui**
hot (touch)	**atsui**	cold (touch)	**tsumetai**
think (flat things)	**atsui**	thin (flat things)	**usui**
thick (cylindrical things), fat	**futoi**	thin (cylindrical things)	**hosoi**
spacious	**hiroi**	limited space	**semai**
cute	**kawaii**	ugly	**minikui**
frightful, frightening	**kowai**	gentle	**yasashii**
difficult	**muzukashii**	easy	**yasashii**
long	**nagai**	short (length)	**mijikai**
delicious, tasty	**oishii**	unsavory (taste)	**mazui**
big, large	**ōkii**	small, little	**chiisai**
heavy	**omoi**	light (weight)	**karui**
interesting, amusing	**omoshiroi**	boring	**tsumaranai**
expensive	**takai**	cheap	**yasui**
high, tall	**takai**	low, short (height)	**hikui**
good	**yoi/ii**	bad	**warui**

Japanese adjectives describe nouns, and they precede
the nouns they describe, just as in English.

heavy book   **omoi hon**

expensive fruit	takai kudamono
small red car	chiisai akai kuruma
This is a short pencil.	Kore wa mijikai enpitsu desu.
This is a big house.	Koko wa ōkii ie desu.
Father buys a big car.	Otōsan wa ōkii kuruma o kaimasu.

Negative I-Adjectives

Negative *i*-adjectives (not big, not delicious, etc.) are formed by changing **_i** to **_ku nai**.

ōkii ringo	a big apple
ōkiku nai ringo	a not big apple
oishii ringo	a delicious apple
oishiku nai ringo	a not delicious apple

Ii, good, is an irregular adjective. *Ii* changes to *yoi* to conjugate.

ii hon	a good book
yokunai hon	a not good book

I-adjectives that do not have their opposite *i*-adjectives are listed below. Some, but not all, colors are also *i*-adjectives.

dangerous	**abunai**	unusual, rare	**mezurashii**
busy	**isogashii**	lonely	**sabishii**
dirty	**kitanai**	enjoyable	**tanoshii**
hard (full of suffering)	**kurushii**	noisy	**urusai**
red	**akai**	yellow	**kiiroi**
blue	**aoi**	black	**kuroi**
brown	**chairoi**	white	**shiroi**

139

This and That: Adjectives

day ***hi***   person ***hito***

There are many words meaning *this* and *that* in Japanese.
Corresponding to the demonstrative adjectives in <u>*this*</u> *book*,
<u>*that*</u> *station*, <u>*that*</u> *person (over there)* and <u>*Which*</u> *apple?* are
kono, ***sono***, ***ano*** and ***dono***. As you will expect from what
you have learned of ***kore***, ***sore***, ***are*** and ***dore*** (as well as
koko, ***soko***, ***asoko*** and ***doko***), the adjective ***kono*** describes a
thing/person/place near a speaker, ***sono*** describes a thing/
person/place near a listener, ***ano*** describes a thing/person/
place away from both a speaker and a listener, and ***dono*** is
an interrogative adjective meaning *which*. They are placed
before the nouns they describe.

this	***kono***	that	***sono***
that (over there)	***ano***	Which?	***dono***

this book (near the speaker)	***kono hon***
that pencil (near the listener)	***sono enpitsu***
that temple (away from the speaker and the listener)	***ano (o)tera***
Which apple?	***dono ringo***

If both a demonstrative adjective and an ordinary adjective
describe a noun, the ordinary adjective follows the demonstrative adjective.

that big person (over there)	***ano ōkii hito***
this small dog	***kono chiisai inu***

This big desk is the teacher's desk.
Kono ōkii tsukue wa sensei no tsukue desu.

That interesting person is my grandfather.
Ano omoshiroi hito wa boku no ojīsan desu.

▶

Note that **kore**, **sore**, **are** and **dore** (and **koko**, **soko**, **asoko**
and **doko**) are pronouns: they are used instead of nouns
and they always stand by themselves. **Kono, sono, ano** and
dono are adjectives: they describe nouns and they are placed
before the nouns they describe.

That person is Hanako.	**Ano hito wa Hanako-san desu.**
That is Hanako.	**Are wa Hanako-san desu.**
May I have that apple please?	**Sono ringo o kudasai.**
May I have that please?	**Sore o kudasai.**
Do you read this book?	**Anata wa kono hon o yomimasu ka.**
Do you read this?	**Anata wa kore o yomimasu ka.**
Which book do you read?	**Anata wa dono hon o yomimasu ka.**
Which do you read?	**Anata wa dore o yomimasu ka.**

You know now that, when two people are talking, a speaker
may ask a listener **kore wa nan desu ka**, *what is this (near
me)?*, meaning something near the speaker. The listener then
answers with **sore wa pen desu**, *that (near you) is a pen*,
since the pen is closer to the speaker than to the listener,
and whenever they are talking about a thing/place/person
away from them both, **are/asoko/ano-hito** is used.

Note that **kore/koko/kono-hito**, **sore/soko/sono-hito** and
are/asoko/ano-hito are used not only in the tangible sense,
but also in an intangible sense. For example, once a speaker
mentions a thing/place/person, it may be referred to as
kore/koko/kono-hito in the rest of his conversation, and it
is translated as *it/he/she*. The listener refers to it by **sore/
soko/sono-hito**, and it is likewise translated as *it/he/she*. **Are/
asoko/ano-hito** can be used to refer to a thing/place/person

▶

somehow far away from them both, in an intangible or a
temporal sense, but it is also translated as *it/he/she*. In the
examples above, ***ano hito*** and ***are, sono ringo*** and
sore, kono hon and ***kore***, and ***dono hon*** and ***dore*** may be
translated as *she, that/it, this/it* and *which* respectively.

Exercise 1

🔊 You will hear an English adjective. Reply with the
corresponding Japanese word. Check your answers on the
recording.

Exercise 2

Convert the following phrases to read "not __."

1. isogashii hito isogashiku nai hito

2. mezurashii tori _____

3. sabishii (o)tera _____

4. urusai inu _____

5. tanoshii hi _____

6. akai ringo_____

Exercise 3

Replace the following two words with one rōmaji word such as
kore, ***koko***, etc.

1. kono hito kochira

2. ano tabemono_____

3. ano gakkō _____

4. kono kissaten _____

5. ano kaisha_____

6. sono kisha_____

Translate into English:

Exercise 4

1. aoi me _____

2. ōkii sutēki _____

3. kono inu_____

4. kowaku nai sensei _____

5. samuku nai hi_____

6. Otōsan wa kaisha e kono kuroi kuruma de ikimasu. _____

_____

7. Natsu watashi to otōto wa yasashii Nihon-go o naraimasu.

_____

8. Anata wa muzukashii hon o gakkō de yomimasu ka. _____

_____

Translate into rōmaji:

9. cold water _____

10. big person_____

11. that (over there) child _____

12. not interesting movie _____

13. This is a long train. _____

I-Adjectives as Complements

Look at the following two sentences with the adjective *big*.

1. This is a *big* apple.
2. The apple is *big*.

The *big* in the sentence 1 is an adjective describing the noun *apple*. The *big* in the sentence 2 is an adjective used as the complement of the sentence, which you are going to study now. ▶

I-adjectives can be used as complements, just like English adjectives.

to be red	*akai desu*
to be lonely	*sabishii desu*
to be warm	*atatakai desu*

Sentences that use *i*-adjectives as complements have the structure

<u>subject</u> *wa* <u>*i*-adjective</u> *desu*.

The apple is red.	*Ringo wa akai desu.*
That dog is frightening.	*Sono inu wa kowai desu.*
The foreigner is unusual.	*Gaijin wa mezurashii desu.*
This place is dirty.	*Koko wa kitanai desu.*
I am hot.	*Watashi wa atsui desu.*

Negative I-Adjectives as Complements

Look at the following two sentences.

1. This is red.   *Kore wa akai desu.*
2. This is a book.   *Kore wa hon desu.*

There is no great difference grammatically between the sentences "This is red" and "This is a book" in English. The negative statements are obtained by putting *not* after the verb *is* for both sentences in English ("this is *not* red" and "this is *not* a book"). But the Japanese *i*-adjectives are very different from English adjectives: they conjugate (change forms), to form negative adjectives.

The negative statement of <u>subject</u> *wa __i desu* is

<u>subject</u> *wa __ku nai desu.*

▶

To negate the sentence that has an *i*-adjective as its complement, the *i*-adjective conjugates while the verb **desu** remains the same. When the complement is a noun, as in sentence 2 above, the noun remains the same while the verb **desu** conjugates. The negative statements for sentences 1 and 2 above are as follows.

    1. This is not red.   **Kore wa akaku nai desu.**
    (adjective **akai** conjugates while **desu** remains unchanged)

    2. This is not a book.   **Kore wa hon de wa arimasen.**
    (verb **desu** conjugates)

The form for the Japanese sentence 1, which has an adjective for its complement, differs from that of the Japanese sentence 2, which has a noun for its complement. The following examples show sentences with adjectives as their complements.

My room is spacious.	**Boku no heya wa hiroi desu.**
My room is not spacious.	**Boku no heya wa hiroku nai desu.**
This book is interesting.	**Kono hon wa omoshiroi desu.**
This book is not interesting.	**Kono hon wa omoshiroku nai desu.**
An American is unusual.	**Amerika-jin wa mezurashii desu.**
An American is not unusual.	**Amerika-jin wa mezurashiku nai desu.**

🔊 You will hear a statement. Reply with the corresponding negative statement. Check your answers on the recording.

Exercise 6

Translate into English:

1. Kono natsu wa atsui desu ne. _____

_____

2. Betty-san no inu wa kitanai desu. _____

_____

3. Kono kudamono wa yasui desu yo. _____

_____

4. Umi no mizu wa tsumetai desu ne. _____

_____

5. Nihon-jin wa mezurashiku nai desu. _____

_____

Translate into rōmaji:

6. Canada is cold._____

_____

7. This is unusual. _____

_____

8. Is Britain interesting? _____

_____

9. Is the school enjoyable? _____

_____

10. My umbrella is not black. _____

_____

Na-Adjectives

So far, you have learned i-adjectives. In this section, you are going to learn the other type of adjective: **na**-adjective. As you can see from the list below, **na**-adjectives end with **na**.

foolish, stupid	**baka na**	clever	**rikō na**
		splendid	**rippa na**
convenient	**benri na**	romantic	**romanchikku na**
inconvenient	**fuben na**		
healthy, hearty	**genki na**	kind	**shinsetsu na**
		quiet, peaceful	**shizuka na**
handsome	**hansamu na**		
strange, suspicious	**hen na**	precious	**taisetsu na**
		famous	**yūmei na**
beautiful, clean	**kirei na**		

Na-adjectives precede the nouns and pronouns they describe, just as i-adjectives do.

kind person	**shinsetsu na hito**
strange person	**hen na hito**

Negative Na-Adjectives

Negative **na**-adjectives (*not* splendid, *not* beautiful, etc.) are formed by changing **na** to **de (wa) nai**.

a healthy person	**genki na hito**
a not healthy person	**genki de nai hito**
a kind person	**shinsetsu na hito**
a not kind person	**shinsetsu de nai hito**

Na-Adjectives as Complements

Na must be dropped when **na**-adjectives are used as complements.

He is odd.   **Ano hito wa hen desu.**
I am healthy.   **Watashi wa genki desu.**

You may notice that the greeting **(o)genki desu ka** is the abbreviation and honorific speech for **anata wa genki desu ka**, meaning *are you healthy?* The reply **hai genki desu** is the abbreviation of **hai watashi wa genki desu**, meaning *yes, I am healthy.*

Negative Na-Adjectives as Complements

The negative of "**na**-adjective (without **na**) + **desu**" is obtained by changing **desu** into **de wa arimasen**. For **na**-adjectives, the verb **desu** conjugates, while the **na**-adjectives do not.

He is kind.   **Ano hito wa shinsetsu desu.**
He is not kind.   **Ano hito wa shinsetsu de wa
                          arimasen.**

This (place) is quiet.   **Koko wa shizuka desu.**
This (place) is not quiet. **Koko wa shizuka de wa arimasen.**

Exercise 7

Convert the following phrases to read "not ___" and then translate them into English.

1. shinsetsu na hito <u>shinsetsu de nai hito</u> <u>not a kind person</u>

2. genki na inu _____

_____

3. yūmei na (o)tera_____

_____

💿 Dialogue 2

Tom: Cute wa rikō desu yo.
           Asa (Cute wa) boku o basu-sutoppu made
           miokurimasu.
           Gogo (Cute wa) boku no kaeri o basu-sutoppu de
           machimasu.
           Cute wa boku no taisetsu na inu desu.
Hanako: Cute wa genki desu ne.
           Yoru Cute wa urusai desu ka.
Tom: Iie (yoru Cute wa) shizuka desu.

miokurimasu   see (a person off)
kaeri   return

Is He Noisy at Night?

Tom and Hanako continue the conversation on Cute.

Tom: Cute is clever!
                In the morning, he sees me off to the bus
                stop.
                In the afternoon, he waits for my return
                at the bus stop.
                Cute is my precious dog.
Hanako: Cute is energetic, isn't he?
                Is he noisy at night?
Tom: No, he is quiet.

Exercise 8

Translate into English:

1. shizuka na (o)tera _____

2. hansamu na hito _____

3. Tarō wa genki na neko desu. _____

_____

4. Kore wa otōsan no taisetsu na hon desu. _____

_____

Translate into rōmaji:

6. healthy cat_____

7. beautiful eyes _____

8. not kind person _____

9. This is a famous picture. _____

10. That is a healthy child. _____

Writing Exercise

Practice the five katakana characters *a, i, u, e,* and *o*

ア, イ, ウ, エ and オ.

a

e

i

o

u

What Do You Like?

Dialogue 1

Tom: (Anata wa) eiga ga suki desu ka.
Hanako: Hai suki desu.
Tom: (Anata wa) nan no eiga ga suki desu ka.
Hanako: (Watashi wa) romanchikku na eiga ga suki desu.
Tom: (Anata wa) tabemono wa nani ga suki desu ka.
Hanako: (Watashi wa tabemono wa) yakisoba ga suki desu.
Tom: (Anata wa) nomimono wa nani ga suki desu ka.
Hanako: (Watashi wa nomimono wa) orenji-jūsu ga suki desu.
Tom: (Anata wa) dono sensei ga suki desu ka.
Hanako: (Watashi wa) rekishi no sensei ga suki desu.

What Kinds of Movies Do You Like?

Tom tries to find out what Hanako likes.

Tom: Do you like movies?
Hanako: Yes, I do.
Tom: What kinds of movies do you like?
Hanako: I like romantic movies.
Tom: What foods do you like? (As for food, what do you like?)
Hanako: I like yakisoba.
Tom: What drinks do you like? (As for drink, what do you like?)
Hanako: I like orange juice.
Tom: Which teacher do you like?
Hanako: I like the history teacher.

I Like: Adjective + Desu

The sentence structure:

<u>indirect subject</u> **wa** <u>grammatical subject</u> **ga** "adjective + **desu**"

is used to express like, dislike or want and describe skills, physical appearances and conditions.

Wa follows indirect subject ("topic" in Japanese grammar) and is translated as "as for __", but becomes a subject in English translation.

Ga follows grammatical subject (subject in Japanese grammar but direct object etc. in English translation).

The sentence is translated
As for (indirect subject) (grammatical subject) *is* (adjective)

Suki Na and Kirai Na

The following **na**-adjectives can help you talk about, and ask others about, likes and dislikes.

likeable   **suki na**
detestable, dislikable   **kirai na**

The literal English translations for **suki na ringo** and **kirai na ringo** are *a likable apple* and a *dislikable apple*. More appropriate English translations for them are *the apple that somebody likes* and *the apple that somebody dislikes*.

The fruit that somebody likes is apples.
Suki na kudamono wa ringo desu.
The carrots are vegetables that somebody dislikes.
Ninjin wa kirai na yasai desu.

Since the above sentences do not state *who* likes apples or *who* dislikes carrots, it is assumed that the speaker is talking about himself. Hence the above sentences imply *I like apples* and *I dislike carrots*.

Negative Forms

The negative adjectives for **suki na** and **kirai na** are obtained just as for other **na**-adjectives: na is replaced by **de (wa) nai**.

the food that somebody doesn't like	**suki de (wa) nai tabemono**
the teacher that somebody does not dislike	**kirai de (wa) nai sensei**
At night, I read the book that I do not like.	**Yoru watashi wa suki de (wa) nai hon o yomimasu.**

Suki Na and Kirai Na as Complements

Now consider the adjectives **suki na** and **kirai na** as complements. Just as for other **na**-adjectives, na is dropped—**suki desu**, *to be likable*, and **kirai desu**, *to be dislikable*—but they use a different sentence structure from other adjectives you learned.

Suki/kirai na is used as a complement in the sentence structure:

<u>grammatical subject</u> **ga suki/kirai desu**

Ga follows the grammatical subject and **suki/kirai desu** is translated as *to be likable/dislikable*.

Ringo ga suki desu.	Apples are likable.
Tenisu ga kirai desu.	Tennis is dislikable.

You have already learned that _*wa* may be used to express
a topic in a sentence and may be translated as *as for _*.
Let us put ***watashi wa*** in the sentence ***ringo ga suki desu:***
watashi wa ringo ga suki desu. The literal translation is
as for me, apples are likable, but of course, *I like apples* is a
more appropriate translation in English.
Here, ***Suki/kirai desu*** uses the sentence structure

<u>(English subject)</u> ***wa*** <u>(English object)</u> ***ga suki/kirai desu***.

Let us consider the sentence ***watashi wa ringo ga suki
desu***, *I like apples*, and insert ***kudamono wa***, *as for fruit*, in
the sentence. Then, we get ***watashi wa kudamono wa ringo
ga suki desu***, *as for fruit, I like apples*. Of course, *I like
apples for fruit* is a more appropriate translation in English.

I like tennis.	***Watashi wa tenisu ga suki desu.***
I dislike carrots.	***Watashi wa ninjin ga kirai desu.***
What do you like?	***Anata wa nani ga suki desu ka.***

The negative of ***suki/kirai desu*** is ***suki/kirai de wa
arimasen***, just as for other ***na***-adjectives.

Betty does not like apples.
Betty-san wa ringo ga suki de wa arimasen.

I Love You

Watashi wa _ ga suki desu is usually translated as
I like _. However, **(watashi wa) anata ga suki desu**,
when spoken to a member of the opposite sex, becomes
a very strong statement and is interpreted as *I love you*
and not *I like you*. Now you know what to say when you
are in love!

Jōzu/Heta Na: I am Good at That

Here is another set of **na**-adjectives.

good (at a particular skill)	**jōzu na**
bad (at a particular skill)	**heta na**

Just as for other na-adjectives, negative adjectives are obtained by replacing **na** with **de (wa) nai**.

a good picture	**jōzu na e**
not a good picture	**jōzu de (wa) nai e**
That good picture is the teacher's picture.	**Ano jōzu na e wa sensei no e desu.**

When **jōzu na** and **heta na** are used as complements, **na** must be dropped, just as for other na-adjectives: **jōzu desu**, to be good (at a skill), and **heta desu**, to be bad (at a skill). **Jōzu/heta desu** follows the same structure as **suki/kirai desu**. The negative of **jōzu/heta desu** is obtained by changing **desu** into **de wa arimasen**, just as for other **na**-adjectives.

Grandfather is good at the Japanese language.
Ojīsan wa Nihon-go ga jōzu desu.
I am not good at tennis.
Boku wa tenisu ga jōzu de wa arimasen.

Hoshii: I Want That

desirable	**hoshii**

Hoshii conjugates like any other **i**-adjective: the negative of **hoshii** is **hoshiku nai**.

the book that somebody wants (a desirable book)	**hoshii hon**
the book that somebody doesn't want (not a desirable book)	**hoshiku nai hon**

> The fruit that somebody   **Hoshii kudamono wa**
> wants is strawberries.   **ichigo desu.**
>
> **Hoshii desu,** *to be desirable/wanted*, follows the
> same structure as **suki/kirai desu** and its negative tense
> is formed just like any other i-adjective complement:
> **hoshiku nai desu.**
>
> I want a red dress.
> **Watashi wa akai fuku ga hoshii desu.**
> I don't want breakfast.
> **Watashi wa asa-gohan ga hoshiku nai desu.**
> What do you want?
> **Anata wa nani ga hoshii desu ka.**

Exercise 1

Write the following sentences in rōmaji using the sentence
structure _ **wa** _ **ga** _ **desu** (or **de wa arimasen**).

Write that you like following things:

1. apple _____

2. tempura _____

Write that you dislike the following things:

3. carrot _____

4. milk _____

Write that you are good at the following things:

5. tennis _____

6. English _____

Write that you are not good at the following things:

7. swimming _____

8. Japanese _____

Write that you want the following things:

9. steak _____

10. TV _____

Questions and Replies

The replies for _ **wa** _ **ga** "adjective + **desu**" **ka** are
hai "adjective + **desu**" or **iie** negative of "adjective + **desu**."

Question   Answer

Anata wa ringo ga suki desu ka.   **Hai suki desu.**
Do you like apples?   Yes, I do.
                                 Iie suki de wa arimasen.
                                 No, I don't.

Ananta wa kore ga hoshii desu ka.   **Hai hoshii desu.**
Do you want this?   Yes, I do.
                                 Iie hoshiku nai desu.
                                 No, I don't.

🎧 You will hear a description of Tom's older brother. Answer
the following questions in rōmaji.

1. Onīsan wa nan no supōtsu o shimasu ka. _____
_____

2. Onīsan wa jūdō ga jōzu desu ka. Iie _____
_____

3. Onīsan wa sumō ga suki desu ka. _____
_____

Exercise 2

Translate into English:

1. suki na hito _____

2. hoshii hon _____

3. kirai de wa nai sensei _____

4. hoshiku nai gohan _____

5. Ringo wa suki na kudamono desu. _____

Exercise 3

▶

6. Watashi wa kirai na hon o gakkō de yomimasu. _____

_____

7. Ano zō wa anata no banana ga hoshii desu. _____

_____

Translate into rōmaji:

8. the teacher whom somebody dislikes_____

9. bad English _____

10. not good Japanese _____

11. the drink that somebody doesn't want_____

12. I like Japanese people. _____

13. For dinner, I want a big steak. _____

_____

14. Whom do you like? _____

Itai, Kayui: That Hurts!

Here are two more adjectives to help you describe how
you are feeling. They use the same sentence structure as
suki/kirai to describe physical conditions.

painful	**itai**
itchy	**kayui**

I have a headache. (As for me, the head is painful.)
Watashi wa atama ga itai desu.

My legs are itchy. (As for me, the legs are itchy.)
Watashi wa ashi ga kayui desu.

Write in rōmaji that you have pain in the following parts of your body, using the sentence structure _ **wa** _ **ga** _ **desu**.

1. head _____

2. leg _____

3. arm _____

4. eye _____

5. stomach _____

Exercise 4

Describing Others with "Adjective + Desu"

These adjectives aren't just for talking about yourself! The same structure as **suki/kirai desu** can be used to describe other people (and animated subjects), using the following vocabulary.

height, stature	**se**
quiet (sound, voice)	**chiisai**
loud (sound, voice)	**ōkii**

Hanako has big eyes. (As for Hanako, the eyes are big.)
Hanako-san wa me ga ōkii desu.

Americans are tall. (As for Americans, the heights are big.)
Amerika-jin wa se ga takai desu.

Makoto has a quiet voice. (As for Makoto, the voice is quiet.)
Makoto-kun wa koe ga chiisai desu.

The above sentences are equivalent to the following sentences.

Hanako's eyes are big.
Hanako-san no me wa ōkii desu.

Americans are tall. (Americans' heights are big.)
Amerika-jin no se wa takai desu.

Makoto's voice is quiet.
Makoto-kun no koe wa chiisai desu.

Exercise 5

Translate into English:

1. Watashi wa onaka ga itai desu. _____

_____

2. Hanako-san wa me ga kirei desu. _____

_____

3. Kirin wa kubi ga nagai desu ka. _____

_____

4. Nihon-jin wa hana ga hikui desu ne. _____

_____

Translate into rōmaji:

5. My arms are itchy. _____

_____

6. I have a pain in my leg. _____

_____

7. My father has big hands. _____

_____

8. Elephants have long noses. _____

_____

Writing Exercise

Practice the five katakana characters **ka, ki, ku, ke** and **ko**
カ, キ, ク, ケ and コ.

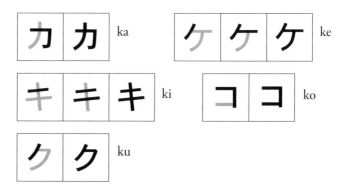

Beautiful, More Beautiful, Most Beautiful

🔘 Dialogue 1

Tom:	Tōkyō wa totemo atsui desu ne.
Hanako:	(Hai) sō desu ne. Aisukurīmu o tabemasen ka.
Tom:	(Boku wa) aisukurīmu ga suki desu.
Hanako:	(Anata wa) dono aisukurīmu ga ichi-ban suki desu ka.
Tom:	(Boku wa) chokorēto ga ichi-ban suki desu.
Hanako:	Watashi wa banira ga chokorēto yori suki desu.
Tom:	Are wa kirai na sensei desu.
Hanako:	(Anata wa ano sensei ga) naze kirai desu ka.
Tom:	Ano sensei wa Nihon-go no sensei desu. Nihon-go wa totemo muzukashii desu.
Hanako:	Anata wa Nihon-go ga jōzu desu yo.

aisukurīmu	ice cream
banira	vanilla
chokorēto	chocolate

Which Ice Cream Do You Like Best?

Tom and Hanko discuss ice cream.

Tom:	Tokyo is very hot, isn't it?
Hanako:	Yes, it is, isn't it? Would you like to eat ice cream?
Tom:	I like ice cream.
Hanako:	Which ice cream do you like best (most)?
Tom:	I like chocolate best.
Hanako:	I like vanilla more than chocolate.
Tom:	Look, that's the teacher I dislike (dislikable teacher).
Hanako:	Why do you dislike him?
Tom:	He is the teacher of the Japanese language. Japanese is very difficult.
Hanako:	You're good at Japanese!

Adverbs

Adverbs describe adjectives, verbs and adverbs. For example, *very* of *a very delicious apple* describes the adjective *delicious*; *quickly* of *I drive quickly* describes the verb *drive*.

A Japanese adverb is usually placed immediately before the adjective, verb or adverb that it describes.

To form adverbs, convert the final *i* of *i*-adjectives into **ku**.

Adjectives	Adverbs
hayai quick, early, fast	**hayaku** quickly, early, fast
ōkii big	**ōkiku** big
omoshiroi interesting	**omoshiroku** interestingly
osoi late, slow	**osoku** late, slowly
takai expensive, high	**takaku** expensively, highly
tanoshii enjoyable	**tanoshiku** enjoyably
yasui cheap	**yasuku** cheaply
yoi good	**yoku** often, a lot

When you are translating a Japanese word that looks like an adverb ending with **ku**, be careful to check that it is not followed by **nai**: a negative *i*-adjective has the form **_ku nai**.

The adverbs formed from *i*-adjectives by changing *i* into **ku** describe verbs only.

Father goes to America often.
Otōsan wa Amerika e yoku ikimasu.

The younger brother eats meals enjoyably.
Otōto wa gohan o tanoshiku tabemasu.

I shall go to the restaurant late.
Watashi wa resutoran ni osoku ikimasu.

I shall sell you this cheaply.
Watashi wa kore o anata ni yasuku urimasu.

Note that the adverb **yoku**, *well*, has many more meanings than just that of converting **yoi**, *good*, into an adverb.

Convert the following adjectives into adverbs.

Adjectives	Adverbs	
1. *hayai* quick early	*hayaku*	quickly, early
2. *nagai* long	_____	long
3. *usui* thin	_____	thinly
4. *yasashii* gentle	_____	gently
5. *tanoshii* enjoyable	_____	enjoyably

Exercise 1

Totemo (or Taihen)

The adverb **totemo** (or **taihen**) is used to mean *very* when it describes a postive adjective or adverb; it is used to mean *a lot* or *much* when it describes a verb.

The following examples show **totemo** describing adjectives, adverbs and a verb respectively.

totemo oishii ringo	a very delicious apple
totemo tanoshii eiga	a very enjoyable movie
Hiroshi-kun wa totemo omoshiroi hito desu.	Hiroshi is a very interesting person.
Ano totemo shizuka na hito wa Kazuko-san desu.	That very quiet person is Kazuko.
Watashi wa kore o totemo takaku urimasu.	I will sell this very expensively.
Hiroshi-kun wa gohan o totemo tabemasu.	Hiroshi eats rice a lot.

Amari

The adverb **amari** is used to mean (*not*) *very* when it describes a negative adjective or adverb describing a negative verb; it is used to mean (*not*) *a lot* or (*not*) *much* when it describes a negative verb.

amari oishiku nai sakana
not very delicious fish

Amari takaku nai sakana o kudasai.
May I have (some) not very expensive fish please?

Kono inu wa amari rikō de wa nai desu.
This dog is not very clever.

Watashi wa gakkō e amari hayaku ikimasen.
I don't go to school very early.

Watashi wa tegami o amari kakimasen.
I don't write letters much.

Exercise 2

Write either **totemo** or **amari** in the blanks.

1. _____ oishii ringo *a very delicious apple*
2. _____ oishiku nai ringo *not a very delicious apple*
3. _____ hayai kisha *a very fast train*
4. _____ hayakunai kisha *not a very fast train*

🔘 More Adverbs

how, in what way	**dō**	so, in that way	**sō**
		soon	**sorosoro**
not yet (used with negative verbs)	**mada**	immediately	**sugu**
		much, many, a lot, plenty	**takusan**
again	**mata**		
a little	**sukoshi**	sometimes	**tokidoki**
already	**mō**	soon, presently, before long	**yagate**
more	**motto**		
why	**naze**	slowly	**yukkuri**
a little while ago	**sakki**		

Would you like to eat more?
Motto tabemasen ka.

Hanako has not come yet.
Hanako-san wa mada kimasen.

Could you (speak) more slowly please?
Motto yukkuri onegai shimasu.

Father buys plenty (of books).
Otōsan wa (hon o) takusan kaimasu.

Why do you go to school this Sunday?
Kono nichi-yōbi ni anata wa gakkō e naze ikimasu ka.

Dialogue 2

Makoto: (Anata wa) Nihon-go de dare to yoku hanashimasu
ka.

Tom: (Boku wa Nihongo de) Hanako-san to (yoku)
hanashimasu.

Makoto: (Anata wa Nihon-go de) Hiroshi-kun to mo yoku
hanashimasu ka.

Tom: (Iie boku wa Hiroshi-kun to) amari hanashimasen.

Makoto: (Anata wa Hiroshi-kun to) naze (hanashimasen
ka).

Tom: Hiroshi-kun wa (Nihongo o) totemo hayaku hanashimasu. Hanako-san wa (Nihongo o) totemo
yukkuri hanashimasu.

With whom do you often speak Japanese?

Makoto asks Tom about his Japanese speaking habits.

Makoto: With whom do you often speak in Japanese?
Tom: I speak with Hanako.
Makoto: Do you often speak with Hiroshi too? ▶

Tom:	No, I don't speak much with him.
Makoto:	Why?
Tom:	Hiroshi speaks very quickly.
	Hanako speaks very slowly.

Exercise 3

Write adverbs in the blanks.

1. _____ watashi wa soko e ikimasu.
   I shall go there <u>immediately</u>.
2. _____ anata wa benkyō o shimasu ka.
   <u>Why</u> do you study?
3. _____ Hanako-san-tachi wa kimasu.
   Hanako and the girls will come <u>soon</u>.
4. _____ mizu o kudasai.
   May I have <u>more</u> water please?

Exercise 4

Translate into English:

1. totemo kirei na doresu _____

2. totemo ōkii hito _____

3. Watashi wa soko e sugu ikimasu. _____

_____

4. Anata wa Hanako-san ga naze suki desu ka._____

_____

5. Pātī ni sukoshi hayaku ikimasen ka._____

_____

Translate into rōmaji:

6. very fast train _____

7. not very cute cat _____

8. Is a big house very expensive? _____

_____

9. My younger brother speaks English very slowly. _____

_____

10. My father will come soon._____

_____

More/Most: Comparative and Superlative

Japanese adjectives do not have comparative (e.g., *larger*) and superlative (e.g., *largest*) forms. Rather, comparative and superlative are expressed using particles or adverbs, as in the English *beautiful, more beautiful, most beautiful*.

Comparative Degree

The comparative is expressed with the particle **yori** *(more) than*. By inserting **C yori**, *(more) than C*, in the sentence structure **A wa** "adjective + **desu**," you express the comparative idea: **A wa C yori** "adjective + **desu**" implies *A is _____-er than C*.

Consider **Tom-kun wa ōkii desu**, *Tom is big*. Inserting **Makoto-kun yori**, *(more) than Makoto*, in the sentence, we get **Tom-kun wa Makoto-kun yori ōkii desu**, *Tom is bigger than Makoto*.

Hanako-san wa kirei desu.	Hanako is pretty.
Hanako-san wa Yōko-san yori kirei desu.	Hanako is prettier than Yoko.

To reinforce the comparison, add the adverb **motto**, *more*, before adjectives. **Motto** is most often translated as *much*.

Tom is much bigger than Makoto.	**Tom-kun wa Makoto-kun yori motto ōkii desu**
Hanako is much prettier than Yoko.	**Hanako-san wa Yōko-san yori motto kirei desu.**

The sentence **A wa B ga** "adjective + desu" expresses the idea: <u>A</u> is <u>adjective</u> at <u>B</u> (e.g. **Tom-kun wa Nihongo ga jōzu desu**, *Tom is good at English*). You can add **C yori** into this construction in two ways:

> <u>**A**</u> **wa** <u>**C**</u> **yori** <u>**B**</u> **ga** "adjective + desu," meaning
> A is _____-er than C (at B)
>
> <u>**A**</u> **wa** <u>**B**</u> **ga** <u>**C**</u> **yori** "adjective + desu," meaning
> B is _____-er than C.

▶

(My) father is good at English.
Otōsan wa Eigo ga jōzu desu.

(My) father is better than I am at English.
Otōsan wa watashi yori Eigo ga jōzu desu.

This is the case of "A is _____-er than C."

(My) father is good at English.
Otōsan wa Eigo ga jōzu desu.

(My) father is better at English than Japanese.
Otōsan wa Eigo ga Nihon-go yori jōzu desu.

This is the case of "B is _____-er than C."

Note that the above sentence **Otōsan wa Eigo ga Nihon-go yori jōzu desu** can also be written as **Otōsan wa Nihon-go yori Eigo ga jōzu desu**. You must determine from the context whether **Nihon-go yori** is compared with **otōsan** or **Eigo**.

Superlative Degree

Superlatives are formed by putting the following adverbs in front of adjectives.

most, best, **ichi-ban** number one	most, best	**mottomo**

Ringo wa yasui kudamono desu. **Ringo wa ichi-ban/mottomo yasui kudamono desu.**	Apples are cheap fruits. Apples are the cheapest fruits.
Watashi wa ichigo ga suki desu. **Watashi wa ichigo ga ichi-ban/mottomo suki desu.**	I like strawberries. I like strawberries most.
Hiroshi-kun wa se ga takai desu. **Makoto-kun wa se ga ichi-ban/mottomo takai desu.**	Hiroshi is tall. Makoto is tallest.

Convert ordinary statements into comparative statements by inserting _ **yori**, *more than* _.

1. Kore wa yasui desu. *This is cheap.*

Insert **are yori**, *more than that*, to get:

Kore wa are yori yasui desu.

This is cheaper than that.

2. Makoto-kun wa hansamu desu. *Makoto is handsome.*

Insert **Hiroshi-kun yori**, *more than Hiroshi*, to get:

_____

Makoto is more handsome than Hiroshi.

3. Ken-kun wa Chūgoku-go ga jōzu desu. *Ken is good at Chinese.*

Insert **Nihon-go yori**, *more than Japanese*, to get:

_____

Ken is better at Chinese than Japanese.

4. Watashi wa yakyū ga suki desu. *I like baseball.*

Insert **tenisu yori**, *more than tennis*, to get:

_____

I like baseball more than tennis.

Bullet Trains
There are three types of **Shinkansen** trains (bullet trains) running from Tokyo to Hakata: in order of speed and elegance, they are called **Kodama**, **Hikari** and **Nozomi**. The **Kodama** is essentially a second-class **Shinkansen**, relatively slow with many stops. The **Hikari** is a first-class train, relatively fast with few stops, and gives a very comfortable ride. The **Nozomi** is essentially "super-first-class," very fast with fewer stops, and a luxurious ride. Announcements on the trains (for stops, snack service, etc.) are made in both Japanese and English, but the **Nozomi** is much more English-speaker-friendly than the **Kodama**.

Dialogue 3

Makoto:	(Anata wa Tōkyō kara Kyōto made) dono kisha de ikimasu ka.
Tom:	(Boku wa) Kodama de ikimasu.
Makoto:	Hikari wa Kodama yori hayai desu yo.
Tom:	Boku wa Hikari de ikimasu.
Makoto:	Nozomi wa mottomo hayai desu yo.
Tom:	Boku wa Nozomi de ikimasu.

Nozomi is Fastest

Makoto suggests that Tom go to Kyoto by Nozomi.

Makoto:	By which train do you go (from Tokyo to Kyoto)?
Tom:	I'm going by Kodama.
Makoto:	Hikari is faster than Kodama!
Tom:	I will go by Hikari.
Makoto:	Nozomi is fastest!
Tom:	I'll go by Nozomi.

Exercise 6

Say the following sentences in Japanese and check your answers on the recording.

1. Hikari is faster than Kodama.

2. Nozomi is faster than Hikari.

3. Kodama is the slowest.

4. Nozomi is the fastest.

Exercise 7

Translate into English:

1. Nihon no ie wa Kanada no ie yori semai desu.

_____

_____

2. Amerika-jin wa Nihon-jin yori hana ga takai desu.

_____

_____

3. Watashi wa chiri ga rekishi yori motto suki desu.

_____

_____

Translate into rōmaji:

4. The mathematics teacher is kinder than the geography teacher. _____

_____

5. This dog is bigger than my younger brother.

_____

_____

6. American grapes are much cheaper than Japanese grapes.

_____

_____

Practice the five katakana characters **sa, shi, su, se** and **so**.

サ, シ, ス, セ and ソ.

 sa

 se

 shi

 so

 su

That Cat is in My Garden!

 Dialogue 1

Woman:	Ima (o)uchi ni otōsan ka okāsan ga imasu ka.
Tom:	(Ima uchi ni) otōsan mo okāsan mo imasen.
	San-ji made ni (otōsan to okāsan wa) depāto kara kaerimasu.
Woman:	Yo-ji ni (watashi wa) mata kimasu.

Is Your Father or Mother at Home Now?

A visitor comes to see Tom's parents while they are out shopping.

Woman:	Is (your) father or mother at home now?
Tom:	Neither (my) father nor (my) mother is at home. They will be back from the department store by 3 o'clock.
Woman:	I'll come again at 4 o'clock.

The Verb "To Be"

There are four different categories of words and expressions for *to be* in Japanese.

1. **Desu** is used to equate one thing with another (*this* is a *book*).
2. To indicate condition, or quality, or characteristics, Japanese uses "adjective + **desu**".
3. The independent verbs **arimasu** and **imasu** may indicate locations/positions.

4. The progressive present tense is expressed by the verb form called **te**-form followed by **imasu** (e.g., **tabete imasu**, *to be eating*; **hanashite imasu**, *to be talking*).

In this lesson, you will learn category 3 above of *to be*.

Position/Location

The following verbs are used to denote position/location.

arimasu   *to be located/to exist* is used to indicate a position/location of a non-living subject.

imasu   *to be located/to exist* is used to indicate a position/location of a living subject.

Arimasu and **imasu** have the sentence structure

<u>place</u> **ni** <u>subject</u> **ga arimasu/imasu**.

The particle **ni** follows the location of the subject and is translated as *at/in*; the particle **ga** follows a grammatical subject (a subject in Japanese, but not necessarily a subject in the English translation).

Koko ni inu ga imasu.
Here is a dog. (At this place, a dog is located.)
Soko ni neko ga imasu.
There is a cat. (At that place, a cat is located.)
Niwa ni okāsan ga imasu.
The mother is in the garden. (In the garden, the mother is located.)

Koko ni hon ga arimasu.
Here is a book. (At this place, a book is located.)
Niwa ni isu ga arimasu.
A chair is in the garden. (In the garden, a chair is located.)
Asoko ni basu-sutoppu ga arimasu.
That (over there) is the bus stop. (Over there, the bus stop is located.)

Shops

Here is a list of shops whose locations you can describe using the sentence structure discussed above. Notice that the suffix -ya is put after nouns to describe shops.

shops	mise		
flower shop	hana-ya	toy shop	omocha-ya
bookstore	hon-ya	bread shop	pan-ya
cake shop	kēki-ya	fish shop	sakana-ya
fruit shop	kudamono-ya	liquor store	sakaya
butcher shop	niku-ya	supermarket	sūpāmāketto
candy shop	(o)kashi-ya	vegetable shop	yaoya

And here are some common utensils, spices, and teas.

rice bowl	chawan	salt	shio
cup	koppu	soy sauce	shōyu
plate	sara	(Indian) tea	kōcha
pepper	koshō	green tea	(o)cha
salt	shio		

Exercise 1

Circle the words that make sense in the blank for the sentence

Daidokoro ni _ ga arimasu.

shio   koshō   satō   otōsan   shōyu   onīsan
watashi   neko   koppu

Circle the words that make sense in the blank for the sentence

Daidokoro ni _ ga imasu.

kōcha   (o)cha   satō   neko   okāsan   sara

Negative Forms

The negatives forms of **arimasu** and **imasu** are **arimasen** (or **nai desu**) and **imasen** (or **inai desu**) respectively. In this book, we use **arimasen** and **imasen**.

There isn't salt (there is no salt) in the kitchen.
Daidokoro ni shio ga arimasen.
There isn't a cat in the garden.
Niwa ni neko ga imasen.

The particle **mo**, which means *also/too*, replaces **ga** or follows **ni**.

Here is the salt.
Koko ni shio ga arimasu.
Here is the pepper also (as well as salt).
Koko ni koshō mo arimasu.

Here is a cat.
Koko ni neko ga imasu.
There too is a cat.
Asoko ni mo neko ga imasu.

There is neither salt nor pepper here.
Koko ni shio mo koshō mo arimasen.

Questions

Interrogatives **dare,** *who*; **doko**, *where* and **nani**, *what*, are used with **arimasu** and **imasu** as well.

Here is an apple.	**Koko ni ringo ga arimasu.**
Where is an apple?	**Doko ni ringo ga arimasu ka.**
What is here?	**Koko ni nani ga arimasu ka.**
Father is in the garden.	**Niwa ni otōsan ga imasu.**
Who is in the garden?	**Niwa ni dare ga imasu ka.**

▶

175

A reply to the question _ **ni** _ **ga arimasu/imasu ka** uses the sentence structure **hai arimasu/imasu** or **iie arimasen/imasen**.

Question	Answer
Heya ni terebi ga arimasu ka.	**Hai arimasu.**
Is there a TV in the room?	Yes, there is.
	Iie arimasen.
	No, there isn't.

Exercise 2

🔊 Listen to the descriptions of someone's grocery shopping haibts. Answer the following questions in rōmaji

1. Okāsan wa doko de kaimono o shimasu ka. _____

_____

2. Sūpāmāketto ni hito ga ōzei imasu ka. (**ōzei**-many people)

_____

_____

3. Sūpāmāketto wa benri desu ka. (Sūpāmāketto wa) fuben desu ka. _____

_____

4. Sūpāmāketto ni oishii pan ga arimasu ka. _____

_____

5. Doko ni oishii pan ga arimasu ka. _____

_____

6. Okāsan wa niku-ya to sakana-ya e mo ikimasu ka._____

_____

Exercise 3

Translate into English:

1. Asoko ni depāto ga arimasu. _____

_____

2. Soko ni Makoto-kun ga imasu._____

_____

3. Niwa ni ōtosan to okāsan ga imasu._____

_____

4. Koko ni shio mo koshō mo arimasu._____

_____

5. Daidokoro ni neko ga imasu. Niwa ni mo neko ga imasu.

_____

6. Koko ni nani ga arimasu ka._____

_____

Translate into rōmaji:

7. Over there, (there) are father's eyeglasses. _____

_____

8. At that fruit shop, (there) are very delicious apples and
oranges. _____

_____

9. In the hospital, (there) are medical doctors and nurses.

_____

10. Betty is not in the garden. (In the garden, there is not Betty.)

_____

11. Where is the bank? _____

_____

12. What is over there? _____

_____

noun + **no** + noun of position

produces an adverbial phrase such as *in front of the house, on the table, under the desk,* etc. For example, **no mae** implies the position in front of, **no ue** implies the upper part of, **no naka** implies the inside of, and so on. Hence, **ie no mae** is literally translated as *the position in front of the house,* which is more appropriately translated as *in front of the house.* In the examples below, the appropriate translations are given, while the literal translations are given in parentheses.

ie no soto	outside the house (outside of the house)
tēburu no ue	on the table (upper part of the table)
heya no naka	in the room (inside of the room)
ie no mae	in front of the house (front part of the house)
tsukue no shita	under the desk (space under the desk)
okāsan no yoko	beside the mother (position beside the mother)
anata no ushiro	behind you (position behind you)

Betty-san to Robert-kun wa karate o ie no soto de shimasu.
Betty and Robert practice karate outside the house.

Okāsan no ushiro ni otōto ga imasu.
There is (my) younger brother behind (my) mother.

Tsukue no ue ni hon ga arimasu.
There is a book on the desk.

Niwa no tēburu no shita ni neko ga imasu.
There is a cat under the table in the garden.

Write either **no** or **de** in the blanks.

1. Cute wa kawa _____ mizu o nomimasu.
Cute drinks water in the river.

2. Cute wa niwa _____ gohan o tabemasu.
Cute eats his meals in the garden.

3. Kisha _____ naka de tabemasen ka.
Would you like to eat on the train?

Exercise 1

🔘 Say the following phrases using the structure _ **no** _ ,
and check your pronunciation on the CD.

1. in the house

2. outside the house

3. near the house

4. beside the house

5. in front of the house

6. behind the house

7. on the desk

8. under the desk

Exercise 2

Exercise 3

Look at the picture and write rōmaji in the blanks.

1. Tsukue no _____ ni hon ga arimasu.

2. Tsukue no _____ ni neko ga imasu.

3. Tsukue no _____ ni isu ga arimasu.

4. Tsukue no _____ ni enpitsu ga arimasu.

Before / After

ato   (time) after
mae   (time) before

"Noun" **no mae/ato** is used to express time before/after "noun." This phrase may be followed by **ni**.

Gohan no mae ni watashi wa te o araimasu.
I wash (my) hands before meals.

Ban-gohan no ato ni watashi wa terebi o mimasu.
I watch TV after dinner.

Translate into English:

1. Kono inu wa toire no mizu o nomimasu. _____

_____

2. Tsukue no ue ni anata no hon ga arimasu yo._____

_____

3. Ie no naka ni otōsan to okāsan ga imasu._____

_____

4. Watashi no otōto wa manga o basu no naka de yomimasu.

_____

5. Gakkō no mae ni byōin ga arimasu. _____

_____

Translate into rōmaji:

6. Buildings in New York City (Nyūyōku) are very tall. _____

_____

7. On the desk, there is a pencil._____

_____

8. In the sea, there are large fishes._____

_____

9. The post office is beside that big department store.

_____

10. What is on the table in the kitchen?_____

_____

Exercise 4

Direction Words

Arimasu is used to ask a direction. Here is a list of words which are associated with directions.

hō	direction (of travel/motion)
hōkō	direction(s)
kōsaten	intersection
tsukiatari	T-junction
dōro	road, way, highway
michi	road, path, way
shingō	traffic light
hantai	opposite
hidari	left
migi	right
magarimasu	turn
norimasu	ride (on)
massugu	straight through
-gawa	- side

Right, Left or Straight?

When you want to mention the point where a turn is to be made (e.g., "turn right at the intersection," "go left at the T-junction") or proceed further ("go straight through the intersection"), the point is followed by **o** as shown below.

Kōsaten o migi e ikimasu/ magarimasu.
Go/turn (to) right at the intersection.

Tsukiatari o hidari e magarimasu/ ikimasu.
Turn/go (to) left at the T-junction.

Kōsaten o massugu ikimasu.
Go straight through (at) the intersection.

Exercise 5

🔊 Look at the map. You are driving a car, going from south-west to northeast. Write and say aloud what you can see at each exit, using the sentence structure _ **ni** _ **ga arimasu**. Check your answers and your pronunciation on the CD.

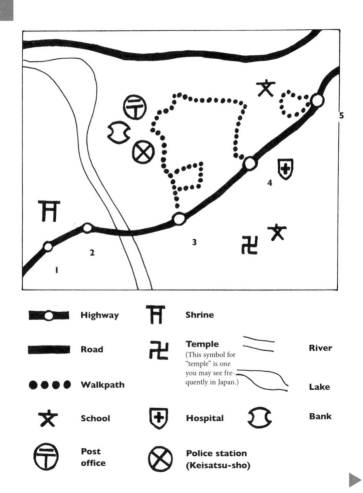

	Highway	卄	Shrine
	Road	卍	Temple (This symbol for "temple" is one you may see frequently in Japan.)		River
●●●●	Walkpath				Lake
文	School	✚	Hospital	⬭	Bank
〒	Post office	⊗	Police station (Keisatsu-sho)	

1. _____

2. _____

3. Hidari-gawa ni _____

Migi-gawa ni _____

Ushiro ni _____

4. _____

5. _____

Say the following sentences in Japanese, and check your answers on the CD.

1. Turn right at the intersection

2. Turn left at the intersection

3. Go straight through the intersection

4. Turn right at the T-junction

5. Turn left at the T-junction

Exercise 6

Translate into English:

1. Watashi wa kono michi o massugu ikimasu. _____

_____

2. Basu wa shingō o migi e magarimasu. _____

_____

3. (Anata wa) ano tsukiatari o hidari e magarimasu. _____

_____

4. San-ban no basu wa Higashi-kōen e ikimasu. _____

_____

5. Watashi wa (o)tera no hantai-gawa de kuruma o tomemasu.

_____

Exercise 7

▶

Translate into rōmaji:

6. (You) go straight through that traffic light. _____

_____

7. (You) turn right at the T-junction. _____

_____

8. This bus will go in the direction of Mt. Atago. _____

_____

9. There is a bread shop at the opposite side of the station.

_____

10. (You) turn left before that hotel. _____

_____

Practice the five katakana characters *na, ni, nu, ne* and *no*.

 and .

 na

 ne

ni

 no

nu

It's Going to Rain Tomorrow

🎧 Dialogue 1

Tom: Konnichiwa. (Yūsuhosuteru ni) heya ga arimasu
ka.

Clerk: Hai arimasu.

Tom: (Heya wa) ikura desu ka.

Clerk: (Heya wa) go-sen-en desu. Asa-gohan to ban-gohan ga tsukimasu.

Tom: (Yūsuhosuteru ni) furo ga arimasu ka.

Clerk: Hai arimasu. (Furoba wa) ik-kai* desu.

Tom: Kyō boku wa (yūsuhosuteru ni) tomarimasu.
Ashita ame ga furimasu ka.

Clerk: Hai furimasu.

yūsuhosuteru   youth hostel

***ichi + kai**, one + floor, has undergone a phonetic change
and became **ik-kai**, first floor.

Do you have a room?

Tom visits a youth hostel.

Tom: Good afternoon. Do you (the youth hostel)
have a room?

Clerk: Yes, we do.

Tom: How much is it?

Clerk: It's ¥5,000. Breakfasts and dinners are included.

Tom: Do you (the youth hostel) have a bath?

Clerk: Yes, we do. It's on the first floor.

Tom: I'll stay tonight (today).
Will it rain tomorrow?

Clerk: Yes, it will.

Intransitive Verbs

Intransitive **V•masu**-verbs (**V•masu**-verbs which do not have direct objects) have the sentence structure

<u>subject</u> **wa/ga V•masu.**

Wa follows a subject responsible for the action.
Ga follows a subject where action is presented as natural occurrence.
You have learned so far that subjects for the verbs of motion are followed by **wa** while the subject for **arimasu/imasu** is followed by **ga**. This lesson will introduce some more subtle distinctions between **wa** and **ga** that determine which particle should be used.

Let's consider **watashi wa yama e ikimasu,** *I go to the mountain.* In this sentence, "going to the mountain" is an action performed by *I.* Because **watashi,** *I,* is responsible for the action, it is followed by **wa**.

Now consider **basu ga kimasu,** *the bus is coming* or *the bus comes.* "The bus coming" is a natural occurrence and hence the subject **basu,** *bus,* is followed by **ga**.

Let's consider **niwa ni otōsan ga imasu,** *father is (located) in the garden.* Because **imasu** means *to be located* or *to exist,* there is no action performed by father: "father" is merely located or exists in the garden. Hence **otōsan,** *father,* is followed by **ga**. The subject may be followed by **wa** only if the subject is responsible for being there. For instance, **koko ni watashi wa imasu,** *I'll be here,* implies a decision of the speaker—**watashi** is responsible for being here and therefore it is followed by **wa**.

Transitive and Intransitive Verbs in English and Japanese

The translation of an English verb into a Japanese verb or vice versa may sometimes be confusing.

I stop a car. *("stop" is a transitive verb in this case)*
A car stops. *("stop" is an intransitive verb in this case)*

In English, the verb *stop* may be both transitive and intransitive. For the sentence with the transitive verb, the direct object of the verb (a car) is stated; for the sentence with the intransitive verb, the sentence is complete without a direct object. The sentence with a <u>transitive verb</u> always states <u>the person responsible for the action</u>, while the action is stated as a <u>natural occurrence</u> in the sentence with an <u>intransitive verb</u>.

In Japanese, transitive and intransitive verbs are almost always two different words. The only exception is **owarimasu** which is both transitive, meaning *finish/end (something)*, and intransitive, meaning *be finished*; the intransitive verb **owarimasu** also has a transitive counterpart **oemasu,** *finish (something)*.

The following example shows that **tomemasu**, *stop (something)*, is a transitive verb while **tomarimasu**, *stop*, is an intransitive verb; but both would be translated as *stop* in English.

Watashi wa kuruma o tomemasu.	I stop a car.
Kuruma ga tomarimasu.	A car stops.

Transitive and Intransitive Verbs in Japanese

Here are some more examaples of words that have two translations in Japanese, although in English they are the same word.

Verbs (Intransitive)		Verbs (Transitive)	
hajimarimasu	begin	hajimemasu	begin (something)
kowaremasu	break	kowashimasu	break (something)
tomarimasu	stop	tomemasu	stop (something)
ugokimasu	move	ugokashimasu	move (something)

Benkyō ga hajimarimasu.	The lesson (study) will start.
Watashi wa benkyō o hajimemasu.	I will start (my) study.
Koppu ga kowaremasu.	The cup will break.
Watashi wa koppu o kowashimasu.	I will break a cup.
Basu ga ugokimasu.	The bus will move.
Watashi wa tsukue o ugokashimasu.	I will move a desk.

More Intransitive Verbs

Here are more intransitive verbs in Japanese.

aimasu	meet	tomarimasu	stay (overnight)
arukimasu	walk		
hatarakimasu	work	furimasu	fall (rain, snow)
nakimasu	cry		
nemasu	sleep	tokemasu	melt
okimasu	wake up	yamimasu	stop (rain, snow)
oyogimasu	swim		

Note that *meet* is usually transitive in English, but the Japanese equivalent **aimasu** is intransitive and follows **ni**.

▶

> **Watashi wa Robert-kun ni hon-ya de aimasu.**
> I meet Robert at the bookstore.
>
> **Watashi wa eki made arukimasu.**
> I'll walk to the station.

The Weather

Below is some vocabulary you can use to talk about the weather.

ame	rain	**tenki**	weather
kumo	cloud	**kumori**	cloudy weather
niji	rainbow	**hare**	fine weather
yuki	snow	**matawa**	or

> **Haru yama no yuki ga tokemasu.**
> In spring, mountain snow melts.
>
> **Gogo ame ga yamimasu.**
> (The) rain will stop in the afternoon.

Write **wa** or **ga** in the blanks and then translate the sentences into English.

Exercise 1

1. Isu _ga_ kowaremasu yo. _The chair will break!_

2. Sorosoro basu _____ kimasu yo. _____

_____

3. Sugu eiga _____ hajimarimasu. _____

_____

4. Kono natsu watashi _____ Eigo no benkyō o

hajimemasu. _____

5. Kisha _____ ugokimasu yo. _____

Exercise 2

🔵 Listen to the phrases on the CD about a father's day at work. Answer the questions in rōmaji.

1. Otōsan wa nan-ji ni okimasu ka. _____

_____

2. Otōsan wa kaisha e basu de ikimasu ka. _____

_____

3. Otōsan wa doko de hatarakimasu ka. _____

_____

4. Otōsan wa nan-ji ni uchi e kaerimasu ka. _____

_____

Exercise 3

Look at the weather forecast, and write the weather forecast for each day.

SUN	MON	TUE	WED	THU	FRI	SAT
日	月	火	水	木	金	土

1. _____

2. _____

3. _____

4. _____

5. _____

6. <u>Kin-yōbi wa kumori matawa hare desu.</u>_____

7. _____

Active and Passive Verbs in English and Japanese

Consider this sentence with a transitive verb: *I eat the apple.*
The verb *eat* is called an active verb because the subject, *I*,
performs the action, *eating.* If you change the sentence to
The apple is eaten by me, the verb *is eaten* is called a passive
verb because the subject, *the apple*, is described as experienc-
ing rather than performing the action. Notice that *apple*,
the direct object of the active verb, is now the subject of
the passive verb. Any sentence with an active transitive verb
(any sentence with a direct object) may be made into a
sentence with a passive verb in English.

Sentences with intransitive verbs cannot be made into passive forms since they do not have direct objects. In some
cases, however, Japanese intransitive verbs are translated as
passive verbs in English. Here are some examples:

dekimasu	be made, be possible	*umaremasu*	be born
tsukimasu	be accompanied, be included	*kikoemasu*	be heard
		miemasu	be visible
kimarimasu	be decided	*okuremasu*	be late
		wakarimasu	be under-standable

Pan ga dekimasu.	The bread is made.
Ongaku ga niwa de kikoemasu.	The music is heard in the garden.
Watashi wa deito ni okuremasu.	I will be late for a date.

Translate into English:

1. Ashita yuki ga furimasu. _____

2. Roku-gatsu ni onīsan no ie ga dekimasu. _____

_____

Exercise 4

▶

3. Otōto wa tomodachi to pūru de oyogimasu. _____

_____

4. Kuruma ga ie no mae de tomarimasu. _____

_____

5. Otōsan wa kuruma no kōjō de hatarakimasu. _____

_____

6. Akachan wa okāsan no ude no naka de nakimasen.

_____

7. Nan-ji ni Nihon no eiga ga hajimarimasu ka._____

_____

Translate into rōmaji:

8. The rain will stop soon. _____

9. When does that mountain snow (snow on the mountain)

melt? _____

10. The mother's voice is heard from the house next door.

_____

11. In summer, I'll swim in the sea. _____

_____

12. The mountain is visible. _____

13. In the spring, I'll meet my uncle in Canada._____

_____

14. In March, the older brother moves to America. _____

_____

Wa or Ga?

Here is a summary of what you have learned so far about **wa** and **ga**.

Desu is an intransitive verb and is used in the sentence structure _ **wa** _ **desu.** In this structure, the subject is always followed by **wa.** Most of the "adjective + **desu**" constructs have the sentence structure _ **wa** "adjective + **desu**"; the subject is also always followed by **wa.** Some of the adjectives (**suki na, kirai na, jōzu na, heta na, itai, kayui, hoshii,** etc.) have the sentence structure _ **wa** _ **ga** "adjective + **desu**". **Wa** follows what is the subject in the English translation (the topic or indirect subject in Japanese) and **ga** follows the object or something else in the English translation (the grammatical subject in Japanese).

Intransitive verbs **wakarimasu** and **dekimasu** (to be discussed in the following section) have the sentence structure _ **wa** _ **ga wakarimasu/dekimasu. Wa** follows what is the subject in the English translation (the topic or indirect subject in Japanese) and **ga** follows what is the object in the English translation (the grammatical subject in Japanese). The verbs of motion, **arimasu** and **imasu,** and some of those listed in the vocabulary in this lesson, are intransitive verbs (they do not have direct objects). They use the sentence structure _ **ga/wa V•masu. Wa** follows the subject when the subject is responsible for the action, while **ga** follows the subject when the action occurs naturally.

Ojisan wa Amerika kara kimasu.	(My) uncle comes from America.
Kisha ga kimasu.	The train comes.

Transitive verbs have the sentence structure _ **wa** _ **o V•masu.** All the transitive verbs are action verbs with their subjects being responsible for the actions; therefore, the subjects are followed by **wa.**

I Understand: Dekimasu, Wakarimasu

Dekimasu, *be made/produced/possible,* and **wakarimasu,** *be understandable,* may be translated as follows.

Pan ga dekimasu.	The bread is made.
Wain ga dekimasu.	The wine is produced.
Eigo ga wakarimasu.	The English language is understandable.

Dekimasu/wakarimasu may be used to express abilities with the sentence structure

> <u>indirect subject</u> **wa** <u>grammatical subject</u> **ga dekimasu/
> wakarimasu.**

Wa follows the indirect subject (subject in the English) and **ga** follows the grammatical subject (object in the English).

Consider **watashi wa Nihon-go ga dekimasu.** It may be translated as *as for me, Japanese is possible.* Of course, *I can speak Japanese* is a more appropriate translation in English. Hence **dekimasu** may be thought of as *can (do)* in English and should be translated according to context.

Watashi wa Nihon-go ga dekimasu.	I can speak Japanese (I can do Japanese).
Watashi wa ryōri ga dekimasu.	I can cook (I can do cooking).

Note how **dekimasu,** *can do,* is different from the verb **shimasu,** *do.*

Watashi wa tenisu o shimasu.	I play tennis.
Watashi wa tenisu ga dekimasu.	I can play tennis.
Watashi wa suiei o shimasu.	I swim.
Watashi wa suiei ga dekimasu.	I can swim.

▶

You may use the following adverb, as well as those learned before, to express abilities in detail.

zenzen   not at all, entirely
                                    (used with negative verbs)

Watashi wa Nihon-go   I can speak Japanese a little.
ga sukoshi dekimasu.

Okāsan wa suiei ga   Mother cannot swim at all.
zenzen dekimasen.

Anata wa Nihon-go ga   You understand Japanese
yoku wakarimasu ne.   well, don't you?

A direct answer to a question _ **wa** _ **ga dekimasu/wakari-masu ka** has the form **hai dekimasu/wakarimasu** or **iie dekimasen/wakarimasen,** just as does **suki/kirai desu.**

Listen as Tom talks about his family's ability with the Japanese language. Write rōmaji in the blanks.

1. _____wa Nihon-go ga mottomo dekimasen.

2. _____ wa Nihon-go ga sukoshi dekimasu.

3. _____wa onīsan yori Nihon-go ga dekimasu.

4. _____wa Nihon-go ga ichiban dekimasu.

Translate into English:

1. Anata wa kono e ga wakarimasu ka.

_____

2. Watashi wa Nihon-go ga sukoshi wakarimasu.

_____

3. Anata wa nan no supōtsu ga dekimasu ka.

_____

4. Otōto wa kuruma no unten ga dekimasen.

_____

5. Ano hito wa Nihon-go ga zenzen dekimasen yo.

_____

Translate into rōmaji:

6. I don't understand Hanako at all.

_____

7. My younger brother can do judo.

_____

8. I cannot study at home.

_____

9. Mother cannot speak English at all.

_____

10. Do you understand Hanako's English?

_____

Taxi   A Japanese taxi driver wears a navy-blue uni-
form with white gloves. Unlike in the West,
a taxi driver in Japan will not come out and
open the door for you; instead he will use a lever at his seat
to open and close the back door (on the left side only). So,
stand out of the way and don't touch the door. He will not
help you with your luggage either. It is not common to tip
taxi drivers in Japan.

Practice the five katakana characters **ha**, **hi**, **fu**, **he** and **ho**.

ハ，　ヒ，　フ，　ヘ　and 木.

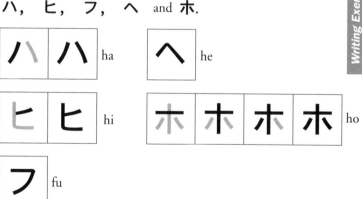

Writing Exercise

22 It All Happened Yesterday

🔵 Dialogue 1

Hanako:	Kinō anata wa nani o shimashita ka.
Tom:	Asa (boku wa) daigaku e ikimashita.
	Hiru (boku wa) daigaku kara kaerimashita.
	Sorekara (boku wa) yakyū o Hiroshi-kun-tachi
	to shimashita.
	Sorekara (boku wa) ban-gohan o tabemashita.
	Yoru (boku wa) terebi o mimashita.
Hanako:	Itsu (anata wa) benkyō o shimashita ka.
Tom:	Kinō (boku wa) benkyō o shimasen deshita.
	Ototoi (boku-tachi wa) sūgaku no tesuto ga
	arimashita ne. Boku wa hyaku-ten o torimashita.
	Dakara kinō (boku wa) asobimashita.
Hanako:	Watashi wa totemo warui ten o torimashita.
	Dakara kinō (watashi wa) sūgaku no benkyō o
	shimashita.
	Korekara (watashi wa) mata benkyō o shimasu.

korekara	from now on	**dakara**	so, therefore
ten	mark, grade	**sorekara**	after that, and then
torimasu	score	**asobimasu**	play, amuse, enjoy
-ten	grade		

What Did You Do Yesterday?

Tom and Hanko talk about what they did yesterday.

Hanako:	What did you do yesterday?
Tom:	In the morning, I went to a class (college).
	In the afternoon, I returned (home)
	from school. After that, I played baseball with
	Hiroshi and the guys.

▶

After that, I ate an evening meal.
At night, I watched television.

Hanako: When did you study?

Tom: Yesterday, I did not study.
The day before yesterday, we had the
math test, didn't we? I scored 100.
So, yesterday, I played.

Hanako: I got a very bad grade. So, I studied math
yesterday. Now, I'll study again.

Past, Present and Future Tense in Japanese

There are two basic tenses in Japanese: present tense and
past tense. Japanese uses the same **V•masu-** verb for the
present and future tenses, but the rest of the sentence makes
the tense clear with a word or phrase such as *tomorrow, now,*
or *next year.*

kinō	yesterday	**kyonen**	last year
kyō	today	**kotoshi**	this year
ashita	tomorrow	**rainen**	next year
itsuka	someday		
sen-shū	last week	**sen-getsu**	last month
kon-shū	this week	**kon-getsu**	this month
rai-shū	next week	**rai-getsu**	next month
mai-asa	every morning	**ototoi**	the day before
mai-ban	every evening		yesterday
mai-nen	every year	**asatte**	the day
mai-nichi	every day		after tomorrow
mai-shū	every week	**kesa**	this morning
		konban	this evening

You may have noticed the following prefixes:

kon-	this *(-getsu, -shū)*
mai-	every *(-asa, -ban, -nen, -nichi, -shū)*
rai-	next *(-getsu, -nen, -shū)*
sen-	last *(-getsu, -shū)*

Forming the Past tense

Form the past tense by converting

1. *desu* into *deshita*
2. *de wa arimasen* into *de wa arimasen deshita*
3. *V•masu* into *V•mashita*
4. *V•masen* into *V•masen deshita*
5. *_i desu* into *_katta desu*
6. *_ku nai desu* into *_ku nakatta desu*

1. **Koko wa hon-ya desu.**   This is a bookstore.
   Koko wa hon-ya deshita.   This was a bookstore.

2. **Ano hito wa Betty-san**   She is not Betty.
   de wa arimasen.
   Ano hito wa Betty-san   She was not Betty.
   de wa arimasen deshita.

3. **Watashi wa pan o tsukurimasu.**   I make bread.
   Watashi wa pan o tsukurimashita. I made bread.
   Watashi wa gakkō e ikimasu.   I go to school.
   Watashi wa gakkō e ikimashita.   I went to school.
   Koko ni hon ga arimasu.   Here is a book.
   Koko ni hon ga arimashita.   Here was a book.
   Ame ga furimasu.   It rains. (Rain falls.)
   Ame ga furimashita.   It rained. (Rain fell.)

4. **Kyō otōsan wa shigoto**   Today, father does
   o shimasen.   not work.
   Kinō otōsan wa shigoto   Yesterday, father did
   o shimasen deshita.   not work.
   Kyō watashi wa gakkō   Today, I do not go
   e ikimasen.   to school.
   Kinō watashi wa gakkō   Yesterday, I did not
   e ikimasen deshita.   go to school.

For the "*i*-adjective + *desu*," form the past tense by replacing *_i desu* with *_katta desu*. The negative past tense is formed by replacing *_ku nai desu* with *_ku nakatta desu*. ▶

5. **Kono ki wa chiisai desu.** This tree is small.
   Kono ki wa chiisakatta desu. This tree was small.

6. **Kono bideo wa omoshiroku
   nai desu.** This video is
   not interesting.
   **Kono bideo wa omoshiroku
   nakatta desu.** This video was
   not interesting.

The past "**na**-adjective (without **na**) + **desu**" is formed by replacing **desu** with **deshita**. The negative past tense is formed by replacing **de wa arimasen** with **de wa arimasen deshita**. In other words, **desu** of the "**na**-adjective (without **na**) + **desu**" conjugates while **na**-adjective (without **na**) remains unchanged.

7. **(O)tera wa shizuka desu.** The temple is quiet.
   (O)tera wa shizuka deshita. The temple was quiet.

8. **Ano hito wa rikō de
   wa arimasen.** He is not clever.
   **Ano hito wa rikō de
   wa arimasen deshita.** He was not clever.

Relative Time

The times listed in the vocabulary on the previous page, except those starting with **mai-,** are called "relative times," that is, the time depends on when "now" is. **Sen-getsu,** *last month*, is a relative time because it means April if it is May now, but it means July if it is August now. When you refer to a relative time, you do not put **ni** after it.

**Sen-getsu watashi wa
Amerika e ikimashita.** Last month, I went to America.

**Watashi wa sen-getsu
Amerika e ikimashita.** I went to America last month.

Exercise 1

Convert the rōmaji sentences from present tense into past tense by filling in the blanks, then translate them into English.

1. Kyō wa yoi (o)tenki desu ne.

Kinō wa yoi (o)tenki <u>deshita ne</u> .

<u>The weather was good yesterday, wasn't it?</u>

2. Kyō no tesuto wa yasashii desu yo.

Kinō no tesuto wa _____

_____

3. Watashi wa Hanako-san ga suki desu.

Kyonen watashi wa Hanako-san ga _____

_____

4. Kyō wa sui-yōbi de wa arimasen yo.

Kinō wa _____

_____

5. Kyō wa samuku nai desu ne.

Kinō wa _____

_____

Exercise 2

🔊 Listen to Tom's essay about his summer vacation.

Answer the following questions in rōmaji.

1. Kyonen no natsu Tom-kun wa doko e ikimashita ka.

_____

2. Tom-kun wa doko ni tomarimashita ka.

_____

3. Tom-kun wa Amerika o ryokō shimashita ka.

_____

4. Tom-kun wa doko ga ichiban suki deshita ka.

_____

5. Mai-nichi Tom-kun wa nani o shimashita ka.

_____

6. Tom-kun wa nani-go o Amerika de hanashimashita ka.

_____

7. Amerika wa suzushikatta desu ka.

_____

8. Tom-kun no natsu-yasumi wa tanoshii natsu-yasumi deshita ka, (Tom-kun no natsu-yasumi wa) tsumaranai natsu-yasumi deshita ka.

_____

Translate into English:

1. Ano hito wa Makoto-kun no onīsan deshita.

_____

2. Kinō Furansu-go no uta ga yūsuhosuteru de kikoemashita.

_____

3. Kyonen no natsu koko ni ōkii ki ga arimashita.

_____

4. Sen-getsu watashi-tachi wa kaimono o Amerika de shimashita.

_____

5. Kinō boku wa isu o otōsan to tsukurimashita.

_____

6. Kinō anata wa nani o ranchi ni tabemashita ka.

_____

Exercise 3

▶

Translate into rōmaji:

7. That was a temple. _____

8. Last year, I went to America by airplane.

_____

9. Yesterday, there was a newspaper on the desk.

_____

10. The long travelling has finished.

_____

11. Last evening, I did not eat dinner.

_____

12. I did not play tennis with Makoto yesterday.

_____

Practice the five katakana characters **ma**, **mi**, **mu**, **me** and **mo**.

マ, ミ, ム, メ and モ.

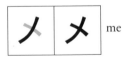 ma

 me

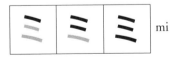 mi

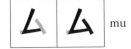 mu

Tomorrow: The Future

Dialogue 1

Tom:	Kyō wa samui desu ne.
Hanako:	Gogo (wa) atatakaku narimasu yo.
	Hachi-gatsu wa totemo atsuku narimasu yo.
Tom:	Ku-gatsu wa (hachi-gatsu yori) suzushiku narimasu ka.
Hanako:	Hai (ku-gatsu wa) hachi-gatsu yori suzushiku narimasu.

It's Cold Today!

Tom and Hanako talk about temperature.

Tom:	It is cold today, isn't it?
Hanako:	It will be warm in the afternoon!
	It will be very hot in August!
Tom:	Will it be cooler in September?
Hanako:	Yes, it will be cooler than in August.

The Future

You may remember that the present and future tenses for **V•masu**-verbs have the same form in Japanese, but there is rarely any confusion between tenses, because the context provides clues.

Rainen watashi-tachi wa Amerika e ikimasu.	Next year, we will go to America.
Ashita watashi wa Eigo no benkyō o shimasu.	Tomorrow, I will study English.

▶

Korekara watashi wa ongaku o kikimasu.	From now (on), I will listen to music.
Korekara okāsan wa gohan o tsukurimasu.	From now (on), (my) mother will make a meal.
Ashita watashi wa e o kakimasen.	Tomorrow, I will not draw a picture.
Ashita ame ga furimasu.	It will rain tomorrow. (Tomorrow, rain will fall.)
Rai-shū gakkō ga hajimarimasu.	Schools will start next week.

In the examples above, you may have noticed that words specifying the future (such as *tomorrow, next year,* etc.) are included in each sentence. In a conversation, once a speaker establishes the time frame, it is not necessary to mention it again, as we saw in the dialogue.

Exercise 1

Circle the words associated with future tense.

ashita   rainen   senshū   raishū   sengetsu   ototoi   asatte

korekara   kinō   kyonen   raigetsu

Circle the words associated with past tense.

ashita   rainen   senshū   raishū   sengetsu   ototoi   asatte

korekara   kinō   kyonen   raigetsu

Translate into English:

1. Asatte wa getsu-yōbi desu.

_____

2. Ashita otōsan to okāsan wa Igirisu kara kaerimasu.

_____

3. Rai-shū onīsan no ie ga dekimasu.

_____

4. Assatte watashi wa ban-gohan o Betty-san no ie de tabemasu.

_____

5. Ashita no eiga wa omoshiroku nai desu yo.

_____

6. Ashita watashi wa anata o eki de machimasu ne.

_____

7. Rai-shū kono hon o anata ni kaeshimasu.

_____

8. Ashita watashi wa tenisu o shimasen.

_____

9. Rai-shū no sui-yōbi ni gakkō ga hajimarimasu.

_____

10. Rai-shū kaimono ni ikimasen ka.

_____

▶

Translate into rōmaji:

11. Tomorrow will be Sunday._____

12. Someday, I will study French.

_____

13. Tomorrow, (my) younger brother and I will go to the temple.

_____

14. What will you do tomorrow?

_____

15. Tomorrow morning, I'll draw a picture of the mountain.

_____

16. Next year, will your grandfather come to Japan?

_____

17. Tomorrow, I will not watch television.

_____

18. Next year, I will buy an expensive blue coat.

_____

19. Next month, a baby will be born to (my) aunt.

_____

20. Tomorrow, I'll put on this dress.

_____

Someday: Ni Narimasu

Unlike **V•masu**-verbs, the verb **desu** does not express the future tense unless the subjects indicate the future, as shown in the examples below.

Ashita wa atatakai desu yo.	Tomorrow will be warm!
Ashita no tesuto wa muzukashiku nai desu.	Tomorrow's test will not be difficult.

The idea of the future tense for **desu** is expressed by using **narimasu,** *to become,* in the future tense. The future tense for _ **wa** _ **desu** is

<u>subject</u> **wa** <u>complement</u> **ni narimasu**

where **wa** follows a subject and **ni** follows a complement.

Watashi wa sensei desu.	I am a teacher.
Raigetsu watashi wa sensei ni narimasu.	Next month, I will be a teacher.

The future tense for _ **wa** "**i**-adjective + **desu**" is

<u>subject</u> **wa** _**ku narimasu.**

The future tense for _ **wa** "**na**-adjective (without **na**) + **desu**" is

<u>subject</u> **wa** "**na**-adjective (without **na**)" **ni narimasu.**

The future tense for _ **wa** _ **ga** "**na**-adjective (without **na**) + **desu**" is

<u>indirect subject</u> **wa** <u>grammatical subject</u> **ga** "**na**-adjective (without **na**)" **ni narimasu.**

Kono inu wa ōkii desu.	This dog is big.
Kono inu wa sugu ōkiku narimasu.	This dog will be big soon.
Yoru gakkō wa shizuka desu.	At night, school is quiet.
Yoru gakkō wa shizuka ni narimasu.	At night, school will be quiet.

▶

Anata wa tenisu ga jōzu desu.	You are good at tennis.
Itsuka anata wa tenisu ga jōzu ni narimasu.	Someday, you will be good at tennis.

The negative future tense may be obtained by changing *narimasu* into *narimasen*.

Hanako-san wa sensei ni narimasen.	Hanako will not be a teacher.
Ashita wa atsuku narimasen.	It will not be hot tomorrow.
Koko wa benri ni narimasen yo.	This place will not be convenient!
Ano hito wa taisō ga jōzu ni narimasen.	He will not be good with gymnastics.

Exercise 3

You will hear sentences telling you what people want to be when they grow up. Match the person with what he/she wants to be.

Tom	a judo instructor
Mari	a nurse
Makoto	a white collar worker
Hanako	a school teacher
Ken	a medical doctor

218

Complete the table below.

Adjective	Meaning	"Adjective + desu"	Meaning	Future Tense
nagai	long	nagai desu	to be long	nagaku narimasu
hoshii	desirous			
muzukashii				
benri na				
rippa na				

🔊 You will hear some questions about the Dialogue. Reply to each question aloud in Japanese, and write your answers below. Check your pronunciation on the CD.

1. _____

2. _____

3. _____

4. _____

Translate into English:

1. Raigetsu Akiko-obasan wa okāsan ni narimasu.

_____

2. Nihon-go no benkyō wa muzukashiku narimasu ka.

_____

▶

3. Itsuka ano hito wa yūmei ni narimasu yo.

_____

4. Pātī no ato daidokoro wa kitanaku narimasu.

_____

5. Anata wa Nihon no rekishi ga suki ni narimasu yo.

_____

Translate into rōmaji:

6. Someday, you will be good at tennis.

_____

7. Will you become a medical doctor someday?

_____

8. Next year, skirts will be short!

_____

9. This tree will not be big.

_____

10. You will like Japanese food.

_____

Christmas and New Year's Day

Most Japanese people do not celebrate Christmas: to them, Christmas is just another day.

Japanese people celebrate New Year's Day, and preparations for the New Year's Day celebration are considerable. The whole nation goes through cleaning rituals as the end of the year approaches. On New Year's Eve, people eat **soba** (Japanese thin buckwheat noodles) either with a dipping sauce or in a hot broth. You are expected to slurp it down your throat loudly. It signifies that the coming year will go smoothly, just as the noodles go through the throat. Celebration of New Year's Day may last from three to seven days, and, during that period, every house is an open house (except those in mourning). People visit their immediate superiors, and those with whom they will associate in the New Year, as well as their families, relatives and friends. Japanese people also send special New Year greeting post-cards, just like Christmas cards are sent in the West. On New Year's Day, people visit shrines to pray to various gods for a prosperous new year. New Year's Day holiday is a great time for children, who get some money from every relative they meet during the holiday.

Japanese Religious Beliefs

Concepts of religion among Japanese people are very different from those of Westerners. The Shinto religion is an ancient native Japanese religion, well established before the introduction of Buddhism in the sixth century. In this religion, people believe that when one dies, his spirit becomes a god who stays somewhere near his descendants. ▶

221

So, people worship ancestors, and every household has a miniature shrine on a small shelf near the ceiling for worshipping the dead. The sun, mountains, wind, rain, trees, rocks and other natural phenomena are believed to be inhabited by individual gods. If worshipped, a god would be benevolent towards people, but, if neglected, a god would be provoked to wrath and might cause a calamity. Shinto has many rituals which have become second nature to all Japanese people, irrespective of their religion. It is customary to hold a ceremony for purifying a building site before any construction may even start. The ceremony is led by a Shinto priest, and is meant to appease the god living there for the massive changes that will be made to the land. Shinto offers no philosophical teaching or moral code, but places great emphasis on fertility and ritual purity.

Buddhism, is the major religion in Japan. Buddhism has moral codes and a complex philosophical system of thought centering on the principles of mercy and humanity. It condemns killing and emphasizes the links among all things. Buddhism stresses the achievement of enlightenment, which may be obtained through faith and behavior. When one finally reaches the state of enlightenment, one is called a buddha. But on the other hand, if one behaves badly, one may be reborn as a lower-ranking creature such as a cat, an insect, or worse, depending on one's entire past behavior. Buddhism, originating in India, came to Japan through China and Korea, where it was transformed by the local religions, and then was also influenced by Shintoism. There are many sects in Japanese Buddhism, and some of them have even adopted the Shinto belief that the dead become buddhas instantly, just as the dead become gods in Shinto.

▶

Christianity was introduced to Japan in 1549, but less than 1 percent of the population is currently Christian.

Daily life in Japan has little connection with religion, except for funeral ceremonies, which are usually Buddhist with deep religious significance. An interesting characteristic of Japanese religions is that they are not mutually exclusive: almost all Japanese families consider themselves as belonging to one of many Buddhist sects, yet you will find some homes with Shinto shrines as well as Buddhist altars. Many Shinto and Buddhist beliefs and practices have merged over the years. In Japan, a person might be a Buddhist, but practice Shinto rituals, might be married at a Shinto or Christian ceremony, which is becoming popular with young couples, and he/she might have a Buddhist funeral.

Practice the three katakana characters *ya*, *yu*, and *yo*.

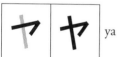

ヤ,   ユ   and   ヨ.

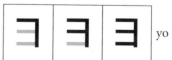

ya

yo

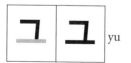

yu

Suggest, or Demand

🔊 Dialogue 1

Hanako:	Ashita Kyōto e ikimasen ka.
Tom:	Hai (Boku wa Kyōto e) ikimasu.
Hanako:	Kyōto ni (o)tera to jinja ga takusan arimasu yo.
Tom:	(Boku-tachi wa Kyōto e) nan de ikimasu ka.
Hanako:	Shinkansen de ikimashō.
Tom:	Nan-ji ni (boku-tachi wa Kyōto e) ikimasu ka.
Hanako:	Jikanhyō o mimashō.
Tom:	Shichi-ji sanjūgo-fun no Kodama de ikimashō. (Boku-tachi wa Kyōto ni) jūichi-ji nijū go-fun ni tsukimasu.
Hanako:	Shichi-ji gojūrop-pun no Nozomi wa jū-ji jūip-pun ni (Kyōto ni) tsukimasu. (Kyōto e) Nozomi de ikimashō.
Tom:	Nozomi wa totemo hayai desu ne.
Hanako:	Nozomi wa tokkyū desu.

jikanhyō timetable   **tsukimasu** arrive

tokkyū super express

Would You Like to Go to Kyoto Tomorrow?

Tom and Hanako plan to go to Kyoto.

Hanako:	Would you like to go to Kyoto tomorrow?
Tom:	Yes, I would.
Hanako:	There are a lot of temples and shrines in Kyoto!
Tom:	How (With what) are we going to Kyoto?
Hanako:	Let's go by Shinkansen.
Tom:	What time do we leave (go)?
Hanako:	Let's look the timetable.
Tom:	Let's go by a Kodama at 7:35. We'll arrive at 11:25.

Hanako: The Nozomi at 7:56 will arrive (at Kyoto) at 10:11.
             Let's go by Nozomi.
Tom: The Nozomi is very fast, isn't it?
Hanako: The Nozomi is a super express.

Let's Go!

By dropping the subject, and converting **V•masu** into
V•mashō, you can produce a polite imperative sentence
that may be translated as *Let's _ .*

Watashi wa hon o yomimasu.	I read a book.
Hon o yomimashō.	Let's read a book.
Yama e ikimashō.	Let's go to the mountain.
Nihon-go no benkyō o shimashō.	Let's study Japanese.
Nemashō.	Let's sleep.
Pūru de oyogimashō.	Let's swim in the pool.

The speaker will suggest things to do together. Write what they
are in English.

1. Let's listen to Japanese music.

2. _____

3. _____

4. _____

5. _____

6. _____

7. _____

Exercise 1

Trains
Japanese bullet trains, known as **Shinkansen**, are world-famous for their speed, safety and comfort. There are six Shinkansen lines and each has two or three different types of trains (faster ones making fewer stops). For instance, for the line between Tokyo and Hakata, there are three types of Shinkansen: they are called **Nozomi**, **Hikari** and **Kodama**, in decreasing order of their speeds. Each Shinkansen has three types of cars (except **Nozomi** which does not have **jiyūseki**): **gurinsha** (first class with reserved seats), **shiteiseki** (reserved seats) and **jiyūseki** (non-reserved seats). **Gurinsha** and **shiteiseki** cost extra. You need two tickets to board a Shinkansen, one for the basic fare (the charge for the distance; it may be used for any other types of trains) and another one for the supplementary fare (the charge for the speed of a particular type of Shinkansen train, and a seat for a particular car).

There are other types of trains for traveling shorter distances. There are as many as four types of trains for each line. They are **tokkyū** (super express), **kyūkō** (express), **kaisoku** (limited express or rapid) and **futsū** (ordinary). Faster trains make fewer stops than slower ones. Whether one uses a **tokkyū, kyūkō, kaisoku** or **futsū,** the fare is usually the same (the basic fare), and some of them have reserved seats, for which there is an additional charge.

Except for the reserved seats, all the tickets may be bought from **jidō-hanbaiki** (ticket vending machines) as well as at **kippu uriba** (ticket selling counters).

Translate into English:

1. Ashita no hachi-ji ni depāto no mae de aimashō.

_____

2. Kono ringo o ojīsan ni agemashō.

_____

3. Ashita tomodachi o hiru-gohan ni manekimashō.

_____

4. Kore o kaimashō.

_____

5. Natsu umi de oyogimashō.

_____

6. Korekara benkyō o shimashō.

_____

Translate into rōmaji:

7. Let's watch TV tonight.

_____

8. Let's study Japanese next year.

_____

9. Let's put on warm sweaters.

_____

10. Let's eat (our) dinner.

_____

11. Tomorrow morning, let's go to the department store by bus.

_____

12. Let's play. _____

Imperatives

You may form an imperative (that is, give an order or instruction) by converting **V•masu** into **V•nasai**.

subject **wa** direct object **o V•nasai**
subject **wa V•nasai**

This form of a sentence is most commonly used by a mother to a child or by a teacher to a student. Since the order or instruction is made by an older person to a younger person, **-san** and **-kun** are often dropped. The subject is usually followed by **wa**.

Robert wa hon o yominasai.	Read the book, Robert!
Betty wa benkyō o shinasai.	Study, Betty!
Tom wa nenasai.	Go to bed (Sleep), Tom!
Anata wa koko ni inasai.	Stay here (Be here)!
Koko e kinasai.	Come here!

Vocabulary

One place you'll see a lot of imperatives is at the doctor's office. Study the following medically-related words and expressions to prepare to read about Tom's visit to a doctor.

dame na	not good	**-do**	degree
iro	color	**kaze**	a cold
kibun	feeling	**kusuri**	medicine

hokenshō	health insurance card
netsu	body temperature, fever
taionkei	clinical thermometer
hakarimasu	measure, weigh
hajimete	for the first time

nomimasu	take (medicine)
yasumimasu	be absent from, rest from, take time off from
(Anata wa) dō shimasu ka.	What will you do (about it)?
(Anata wa) dō shimashita ka.	What's wrong/happened/ the-matter (with you)?

Dialogue 2

Tom: Sumimasen. (Boku wa) atama ga itai desu.

Nurse: Kono byōin wa hajimete desu ka.

Tom: Hai.

Nurse: (Anata wa) hokenshō ga arimasu ka.

Tom: Hai. Kore (wa boku no hokenshō) desu.

Nurse: (Anata wa) kao (no) iro ga yoku nai desu ne.
Netsu o hakarimashō.

***

Doctor: (Anata wa) dō shimashita ka.

Tom: (Boku wa) atama ga itai desu.
(Boku wa) netsu ga arimasu.
(Boku wa) kibun ga warui desu.

Doctor: Taionkei o kudasai. (Anata wa) netsu ga
san-jū hachi-do arimasu.
Kore wa kaze desu. Kyō daigaku o yasuminasai.
Ie de nenasai. Mizu o takusan nominasai.
Furo wa dame desu.
Kyō to ashita kono kusuri o nominasai.

Tom: Dōmo arigatō gozaimashita. Sayōnara.

I Don't Feel Well

Tom visits a doctor.

Tom:	Excuse me. I have a headache.
Nurse:	Is this (your) first time in this hospital?
Tom:	Yes.
Nurse:	Do you have a health insurance card?
Tom:	Yes. This is it.
Nurse:	You don't look well, do you?
	Let's take (measure) (your) temperature.

***

Doctor:	What's wrong?
Tom:	I have a headache.
	I have a fever.
	I feel bad (I have bad feeling).
Doctor:	May I have the thermometer please? You have a temperature of 38 degrees Celsius. This is a cold. Stay home (be absent) from college today! Sleep at home! Drink plenty of water! Don't take a bath (a bath is not good). Take this medicine today and tomorrow!
Tom:	Thank you very much. Good-bye.

Exercise 3

🔘 You will hear some commands. Write what they are in English.

1. _Get well fast!_

2. _____

3. _____

4. _____

5. _____

6. _____

You will hear some questions about Dialogue 2. Reply to each question aloud in Japanese, and write down your answers. Check your pronunciation on the CD.

1. _____

2. _____

3. _____

4. _____

Translate into English:

1. Amy wa tegami o heya de kakinasai.

_____

2. Robert wa miruku o neko ni agenasai.

_____

3. Ashita Kimi to Betty wa gakkō e basu de ikinasai.

_____

4. Tom wa soto de asobinasai.

_____

5. Betty wa Furansu-go no benkyō o shinasai.

_____

▶

Translate into rōmaji:

8. Betty, clean your room!

_____

9. Go to school, Makoto!

_____

10. Eat the tomato, Robert!

_____

11. Kimi, come here!

_____

12. Before a meal, wash your hands, Tom!

Writing Exercise

Practice the five katakana characters **ra**, **ri**, **ru**, **re**, and **ro**.

ラ, リ, ル, レ and ロ.

 ra

 re

 ri

 ro

 ru

Some and Any

Dialogue 1

Makoto:	Nani ka tabemasen ka.
Hanako:	(Watashi wa) nan demo tabemasu yo.
Tom:	Boku wa nani mo tabemasen.
	(Boku wa) onaka ga ippai desu.
	Sakki (boku wa) hiru-gohan o tabemashita.
	(Boku wa yakisoba o) ippai tabemashita.
Makoto:	Korekara nani ka minna de shimasen ka.
Hanako:	(Watashi wa) nan demo shimasu yo.
Tom:	Boku wa nani mo shimasen.
	Korekara boku wa uchi e kaerimasu.
	Dareka boku no uchi e kimasu.
Makoto:	Ashita dokoka e minna de ikimasen ka.
Hanako:	(Watashi wa) doko e demo ikimasu.
	Atago-yama wa dō desu ka.
Tom:	Boku wa doko e mo ikimasen.
	Ashita (boku wa) isogashii desu.

ippai   full, plenty

I'm Full

Makoto suggests activities to Hanako and Tom. Hanako is very agreeable while Tom is not.

Makoto:	Would you like to eat something?
Hanako:	I'll eat anything!
Tom:	I won't eat anything. I'm full. A little while ago, I ate (my) lunch. I ate plenty.
Makoto:	Would you like to do something (from) now, with all of us?
Hanako:	I'll do anything!

▶

Tom: I won't (do anything). I'll go back to (my) house
            (from) now. Somebody's coming to my house.

Makoto: Would you like to go somewhere tomorrow,
            with all of us?

Hanako: I'll go anywhere. How about Mt. Atago?

Tom: I won't go anywhere. I'm busy tomorrow.

Interrogatives

Since interrogatives are the starting point of this lesson,
let's review the interrogatives you have learned so far.

dare	who	**dore**	which one
itsu	when	**doko**	where
nan/nani	what	**dono**	"thing/person" which thing/person

Remember that **nan** is used before a word starting
with n/t/d; **nani** is used in all other cases.

The Particles Ka, Demo, and Mo

Some: Interrogative + **KA** + Positive Verb

"Interrogatives + **ka** + positive verbs" form the following
expressions:

dareka	somebody	**doreka**	something
itsuka	someday	**dokoka**	somewhere
dono "thing/person" **ka**	some "thing/person"		
nanika	something		

▶

Any: Interrogative + **DEMO** + Positive Verb

"Interrogatives + **demo** + positive verbs" form the following expressions:

dare demo	anyone, everyone	**dore demo**	anything
itsu demo	anytime	**doko demo**	anywhere
dono "noun" **demo**	any "noun"		everywhere
nan demo	anything, everything		

(Not) Any: Interrogative + **MO** + Negative Verb

"Interrogatives + **mo** + negative verbs" form the following expressions:

dare mo	(not) anyone	**dore mo**	(not) any of them
itsu mo	(not) anytime	**doko mo**	(not) anywhere
dono "noun" **mo**	(not) any "noun"		
nani mo	(not) anything		

Forming Sentences with Some and Any

As with other question words, to form sentences *some* and *any,* start with a "basic statement" and find the word that will be replaced by *some* or *any.* Check the particle following the word, and follow the rules below.

1. If the word you are replacing is followed by the particle **wa/ga/o,** the particle must be dropped.

2. If the word you are replacing is followed by the particle **ni/e** and if the expression you are replacing it with ends with **demo/mo,** the particle **ni/e** must be put in between the interrogative word and **demo/mo** of the expression.

3. If the word you are replacing is followed by the particle **ni/e** and if the expression ends with **ka,** **ni/e** follows the **ka** of the expression. ▶

The above rules sound complicated. It is much easier to see what they mean by going through the following examples. Let's start with "basic statements".

Consider a basic statement **Watashi wa ringo o tabemasu,** *I eat an apple.*

We want to change *I eat an apple* into *I eat something, I eat anything* and *I do not eat anything.* **Ringo** is the word to be replaced with the expressions *something, anything* and *(not) anything.* Because **ringo** is a "thing," **nani/nan** is the interrogative word we need. Hence, to replace **ringo,** we have expressions **nanika,** *something;* **nan demo,** *anything* and **nani mo,** *(not) anything.* Since **ringo** is followed by **o, o** must be omitted from the new sentences with the expressions (rule 1).

Putting it all together, we get:

Watashi wa ringo o tabemasu.	I eat an apple.
Watashi wa nanika tabemasu.	I eat something.
Watashi wa nan demo tabemasu.	I eat anything.
Watashi wa nani mo tabemasen.	I do not eat anything.

Note that **nani mo** must be followed by a negative verb to mean *(not) anything.*

Let's do the same thing with another sentence, **Watashi wa eki e ikimasu,** *I will go to the station.*

We want to change *I will go to the station* into *I will go somewhere, I will go anywhere* and *I will not go anywhere.* **Eki** is the word to be replaced. Because **eki** is a "place," **doko** is the interrogative word to be used. Hence we have expressions **dokoka**, *somewhere*; **doko demo**, *anywhere*, and **doko mo**, *(not) anywhere* to replace **eki**.

Consider the expression **dokoka**, *somewhere*, first. Since **eki** is followed by **e** and the expression ends with **ka**, **e** must follow **ka** (rule 3). Hence we get: **Watashi wa dokoka e ikimasu**, *I will go somewhere*.

Now consider the expression **doko demo**, *anywhere*. Using rule 2, **e** must be put in between **doko** and **demo** in the new sentence. Hence we get: **Watashi wa doko e demo ikimasu**, *I will go anywhere*.

Now consider the expression **doko mo**, *(not) anywhere*. Using rule 2, **e** must be put in between **doko** and **mo**. Changing the positive verb into the negative verb, we get: **Watashi wa doko e mo ikimasen**, *I will not go anywhere*.

Say the following words aloud in Japanese, and check your pronunciation on the CD.

1. somebody
2. somewhere
3. someday
4. anyone
5. anywhere
6. anytime
7. (not) anyone
8. (not) anywhere
9. (not) anytime

Exercise 1

Exercise 2

Translate into rōmaji:

1. I will read these books. <u>Watashi wa kono hon o yomimasu.</u>

I will read some books. _____

I will read any book. _____

I will not read any book. _____

2. I will buy this. <u>Watashi wa kore o kaimasu.</u>

I will buy something. _____

I will buy anything. _____

I will not buy anything. _____

3. I will give this to you. <u>Watashi wa kore o anata ni agemasu.</u>

I will give this to somebody. _____

I will give this to anybody. _____

I will not give this to anybody. _____

Exercise 3

Translate into English:

1. Watashi wa nani mo hoshiku nai desu.

_____

2. Watashi wa dore mo kaimasen. _____

_____

3. Nanika nomimasen ka. _____

_____

4. Watashi wa doreka yomimasu. _____

_____

5. Dareka kono video o mimasen ka. _____

_____

6. Dare mo yama e ikimasen deshita. _____

_____

7. Itsu demo watashi wa tenisu o shimasu yo! _____

_____

Translate into rōmaji:

8. This dog eats anything._____

9. I won't buy any fruit. _____

_____

10. Would you like to go somewhere? _____

_____

11. I did not see anything. _____

_____

12. I will not buy any dress. _____

_____

13. Makoto does not come to a party ever (any time). _____

_____

14. Would you like to go to a mountain someday?

_____

Practice the three katakana characters **wa**, **wo** and **n**.

ワ， ヲ and ン.

wa

wo

n

Note: This stroke is
drawn from the lower
end to the higher end.

Wishes

 Dialogue 1

Hanako: Ashita yama e ikimasen ka.
Tom: (Boku wa yama e) ikitai desu.
 (Boku wa) yama de e ga kakitai desu.
Hanako: Watashi wa hana ga mitai desu.
 (Watashi wa) tori no koe mo* kikitai desu.
 Nan-ji ni (watashi-tachi wa) ikimasu ka.
Tom: Asa-gohan no ato wa dō desu ka.
Hanako: Nan-ji ni (anata wa) asa-gohan o tabemasu ka.
Tom: Shichi-ji ni (boku wa asa-gohan o) tabemasu.
Hanako: Hachi-ji ni ie o demashō.
 Watashi wa (watashi-tachi no)
 (o)bentō o tsukurimasu.
Tom: (Boku-tachi wa) dono yama e ikimasu ka.
Hanako: Atago-yama wa dō desu ka.
Tom: (Sore wa) ii desu ne.
Hanako: Korekara watashi wa (o)bentō o tsukurimasu.
 Dewa mata ashita.

***

Tom: Yama wa kirei desu ne.
 (Boku-tachi wa) yoku arukimashita ne.
 (Anata wa) tsukaremashita ka.
Hanako: Iie (Watashi wa tsukaremasen deshita).
 (Watashi wa) onaka ga sukimashita.
 (Watashi wa) (o)bentō ga tabetai desu.
Tom: (O)bentō o tabemashō.

sukimasu	be empty, not to be crowded
bentō	meal in a box
tsukaremasu	to be tired

* When **mo,** also/too, refers to the word followed by **ga**, **ga** is ommitted.

Would You Like to Go to a Mountain Tomorrow?

Hanako and Tom go on a trip to a mountain.

Hanako:	Would you like to go to a mountain tomorrow?
Tom:	I'd like to.
	I want to draw a picture on the mountain.
Hanako:	I want to see flowers. I want to listen to the
	cries of birds too. What time will (do) we go?
Tom:	How about after breakfast?
Hanako:	What time do you eat (your) breakfast?
Tom:	I eat at 7 o'clock.
Hanako:	Let's leave (our) houses at 8 o'clock.
	I will make our lunch (in boxes).
Tom:	To which mountain are we going?
Hanako:	How about Mt. Atago?
Tom:	That's good, isn't it?
Hanako:	Right now (from now) I will make our lunch
	(in boxes). See you tomorrow.

***

Tom:	The mountain is beautiful, isn't it?
	We walked a lot, didn't we? Did you get tired?
Hanako:	No, I didn't. I am hungry
	(As for me, the stomach is empty).
Tom:	I want to eat lunch. Let's eat.

I Want To: V·tai Desu

Sentences with transitive verbs, _ **wa** _ **o V•masu,** may be
transformed to express wishes by changing **o** into **ga** and
V•masu into **V•tai desu.**

<u>subject</u> **wa** <u>direct object</u> **ga V•tai desu**

Sentences with intransitive verbs, _ **wa/ga V•masu,** may be
transformed to express wishes by changing **ga** into **wa** and
V•masu into **V•tai desu.**

<u>subject</u> **wa V•tai desu**

Japanese verbs **V•tai desu** may be translated as *want to _.*

▶

Watashi wa hon o yomimasu.	I read a book.
Watashi wa hon ga yomitai desu.	I want to read a book.
Okāsan wa ryokō o shimasu.	Mother travels.
Okāsan wa ryokō ga shitai desu.	Mother wants to travel.
Watashi wa nemasu.	I sleep.
Watashi wa netai desu.	I want to sleep.
Koko ni neko ga imasu.	A cat is here.
Koko ni watashi wa itai desu.	I want to be here.

In the above example, *want to be* here expresses "my desire". Therefore, the subject is not followed by **ga,** which follows a subject when the action is stated as a natural occurrence.

Anata wa nani ga nomitai desu ka.	What do you want to drink?
Anata wa nani ga shitai desu ka.	What do you want to do?
Anata wa dono hon ga yomitai desu ka.	Which book do you want to read?
Anata wa doko e ikitai desu ka.	Where do you want to go?

When an expression "interrogative + **ka/demo/mo** (e.g. **dareka**, **dokoka**, **doreka**, etc.)" is used, the rules you learned last chapter about particles apply.

Anata wa nanika tabetai desu ka.	Do you want to eat something?
Anata wa dokoka e ikitai desu ka.	Do you want to go somewhere?
Watashi wa doko e demo ikitai desu.	I want to go anywhere.
Dareka nanika tabetai desu ka.	Does somebody want to eat something?

I Don't Want To: V·taku Nai Desu

<u>subject</u> **wa** <u>direct object</u> **ga/o V·taku nai desu**

You may make negative statements by converting **V·tai desu** into either **V·taku arimasen** or **V·taku nai desu**. We will use **V·taku nai desu** in this book. The direct object may be followed by either **ga** or **o**.

Watashi wa hon ga/o yomitaku nai desu.	I do not want to read the book.
Watashi wa Eigo ga/o naraitaku nai desu.	I do not want to learn English.
Tarō-kun wa sumō ga/o shitaku nai desu.	Taro does not want to do sumo.
Otōto wa arukitaku nai desu.	The younger brother does not want to walk.

A direct answer to a question _ **wa** _ **ga** _**tai desu ka** is either **hai _tai desu** or **iie _taku nai desu**.

Complete the table below.

V·masu	Meaning	"Want to" Form	"Don't Want to" Form
naraimasu	learn	naraitai desu	naraitaku nai desu
okurimasu			
shimasu			
aimasu			
kimasu			

Exercise 1

Exercise 2

🔘 You will hear what someone wants to do. Write what it is in English.

1. _____

2. _____

3. _____

4. _____

5. _____

Exercise 3

Translate into English:

1. Anata wa dono zasshi ga yomitai desu ka.

_____

2. Ima watashi wa nakitai desu. _____

_____

3. Onīsan wa kawa de oyogitai desu. _____

_____

4. Kyō watashi wa ban-gohan ga/o tabetaku nai desu. _____

_____

5. Watashi wa benkyō ga/o shitaku nai desu. _____

_____

Translate into rōmaji:

6. I want to watch a video tonight. _____

_____

7. I want to eat steak for dinner. _____

_____

8. I want to walk. _____

_____

_____

9. That cat wants to go out from the room. _____

_____

_____

10. Mother wants to buy an Italian handbag. _____

_____

_____

I Wanted To: _takatta Desu

You can convert to the past tense by changing _**tai desu**
into _**takatta desu.**

Watashi wa hon ga yomitakatta desu.	I wanted to read a book.
Watashi wa Amerika e ikitakatta desu.	I wanted to go to America.
Watashi wa ryokō ga shitakatta desu.	I wanted to travel.
Amerika ni watashi wa itakatta desu.	I wanted to be in America.
Anata wa nani ga nomitakatta desu ka.	What did you want to drink?
Anata wa nani ga shitakatta desu ka.	What did you want to do?
Anata wa dokoka e ikitakatta desu ka.	Did you want to go somewhere?

245

Exercise 4

Listen to the phrases on the CD. Convert the sentences into negative statements, write them in rōmaji, and say them aloud. Check your pronunciation on the CD.

1. _____

2. _____

3. _____

4. _____

5. _____

Exercise 5

Translate into English:

1. Watashi wa yama no e ga kakitakatta desu.

_____

2. Kyonen ojīsan wa Amerika e kaeritakatta desu.

_____

3. Natsu-yasumi ni onēsan wa hatarakitakatta desu.

_____

4. Watashi wa machi de kaimono ga shitakatta desu._____

_____

Translate into rōmaji:

5. I wanted to go to England last year.

_____

6. My mother wanted to buy a very expensive dress.

_____

7. I wanted to drive a car.

_____

8. I wanted to drink coffee.

_____

I Didn't Want To: _taku Nakatta Desu

You can form the negative past tense by changing _taku
nai desu into _taku nakatta desu (or by changing _taku
arimasen into _taku arimasen deshita). The direct object
may be followed by either ga or o.

Kinō watashi wa benkyō ga/o shitaku nakatta desu.	Yesterday, I did not want to study.
Imōto wa ban-gohan ga/o tabetaku nakatta desu.	The younger sister did not want to eat an evening meal.
Watashi wa Amerika kara kaeritaku nakatta desu.	I did not want to return from America.
Onīsan wa daigaku e ikitaku nakatta desu.	The elder brother did not want to go to the university.
Robert-kun wa kekkon shitaku nakatta desu.	Robert did not want to get married.

Listen to the phrases on the CD. Convert the
sentences into the past tense and write them below.

1. _____

2. _____

3. _____

Exercise 6

▶

247

4. _____

5. _____

Exercise 7

Translate into English:

1. Kyonen watashi wa Nihon e kitaku nakatta desu.

_____

2. Watashi wa kisha kara oritaku nakatta desu.

_____

3. Otōto wa Furansu-go ga/o naraitaku nakatta desu.

_____

4. Otōsan wa kono kuruma ga/o kaitaku nakatta desu.

_____

Translate into rōmaji:

5. I did not want to go to Germany.

_____

6. I did not want to invite Robert to my birthday party.

_____

7. I did not want to meet you.

_____

8. Yesterday, my younger sister did not want to study math.

_____

Adjectives

🔵 Dialogue 1

Hanako: (Anata wa) tomato to kyūri no sandoicchi ga
tabetai desu ka. (Anata wa) tamago no sandoicchi
ga tabetai desu ka.

Tom: (Boku wa) tamago (no sandoicchi) ga tabetai
desu.

Hanako: (Anata wa) mizu ga nomitai desu ka. (Anata wa)
jūsu ga nomitai desu ka.

Tom: (Boku wa) jūsu ga nomitai desu.
***

Tom: Asoko ni mezurashii tori ga imasu.
Kyonen boku wa Nihon e kitaku nakatta desu.
Boku wa Nihon ga kirai deshita. Ima boku wa
Nihon ga dai-suki desu.

dai-kirai na	very dislikable
dai-suki na	very likable
tamago	egg

I like Egg Sandwiches

Tom and Hanako are about to eat the boxed lunches.

Hanako: Do you want to eat a tomato and cucumber
sandwich, or (do you want to eat) an egg
sandwich?

Tom: I want to eat egg.

Hanako: Do you want to drink water or juice?

Tom: I want to drink juice.
***

Tom: There is a rare bird over there.
Last year, I did not want to come to Japan.
I disliked Japan. Now, I like Japan very much.

Adjective Clauses

_tai may act as an adjective clause by itself and it precedes the word it describes. It is translated as *which/when/where/ that (somebody) wants to _*. The subject of the adjective clause is the same as that of the main clause.

koto	thing (abstract)	**mono**	thing (article)
keshō	make-up	**toki**	time, moment
mukashi	long time ago	**tokoro**	place

tabetai okashi	the candy which (somebody) wants to eat
shitai koto	the thing that (somebody) wants to do
ikitai toki	the moment when (somebody) wants to go
ikitai tokoro	the place where (somebody) wants to go

Tabetai, **shitai** and **ikitai**, above, describe the nouns **okashi**, **koto**, **toki** and **tokoro**, and they may be translated as *that/when/where somebody wants to eat/do/go*. Notice that the translation for the adjective clauses starts with *that, when* and *where* according to the nouns they describe.

Forming Sentences with Adjective Clauses

The easiest way to make a sentence with an adjective clause is to first make a sentence without the adjective clause, and then insert the adjective clause in front of the noun it describes. Let's make the sentence *I buy the fruit that I want to eat*. First, consider *I buy the fruit*: **Watashi wa kudamono o kaimasu**. Insert **tabetai**, *that I want to eat*, in front of **kudamono** to get **Watashi wa tabetai kudamono o kaimasu**, *I buy the fruit that I want to eat*.

The following examples show adjective clauses in sentences. Notice that the subjects of the adjective clauses are the same as those of the main clauses. For example, in the last three sentences, **yomitai hon** is translated as *the book that I want* *to read*, *the book that you want to read* and *the book that she wants to read*, respectively, because the subjects of the main clauses are **watashi**, **Miki** (implying *you*) and **Miki-san** (implying *she*), respectively.

Watashi wa tabetai mono o kaimasu.
I buy what I want to eat.
(I buy the things that I want to eat.)

Watashi wa ikitai tokoro e ikimasu.
I go where I want.
(I go to the place where I want to go.)

Ikitai toki ni ikinasai.
Go when you want.
(Go at the moment when you want to go.)

Kaitai fuku wa takai desu.
The dress that I want to buy is expensive.

Watashi wa yomitai hon o yomimasu.
I read the book that I want to read.

Miki wa yomitai hon o yominasai.
Miki, read the book that you want to read.

Miki-san wa yomitai hon o yomimasu.
Miki reads the book that she wants to read.

Negatives and Past Tense

_taku nai, **_takatta** and **_taku nakatta** are adjective clauses for the negative present, past and negative past, respectively.

yomitai hon	the book that (somebody) wants to read
yomitaku nai hon	the book that (somebody) does not want to read
yomitakatta hon	the book that (somebody) wanted to read
yomitaku nakatta hon	the book that (somebody) did not want to read

> **Kaitai kutsu wa totemo takai desu.**
> The shoes that I want to buy are very expensive.
>
> **Kinō onīsan wa ikitakatta Amerika e ikimashita.**
> Yesterday, (my) older brother went to America, where he wanted to go.
>
> **Watashi wa kaitaku nakatta takai kutsu o kaimashita.**
> I bought the expensive shoes, which I did not want to buy.

Exercise 1

Say the following phrases aloud in Japanese and write them below. Check your answers on the CD.

1. when (I) want to go _____

2. when (I) do not want to go _____

3. when (I) wanted to go _____

4. when (I) did not want to go _____

5. the person (I) want to meet _____

6. the person (I) do not want to meet_____

7. the person (I) wanted to meet_____

8. the person (I) did not want to meet _____

Exercise 2

You will hear some adjective clauses in Japanese. Match the phrase you hear with the correct English translation.

1. _____   **a.** the thing that I want to eat

2. _____   **b.** the thing that I do not want to eat

3. _____   **c.** the thing that I wanted to eat

4. _____   **d.** the thing that I did not want to eat

5. _____   **e.** the place I want to go

6. _____   **f.** the place I do not want to go

7. _____   **g.** the place I wanted to go

8. _____   **h.** the place I did not want to go

Translate into English:

1. Watashi wa shitai koto ga arimasen. _____

_____

2. Koko wa kitakatta tokoro desu. _____

_____

3. Aitakatta hito wa Amerika e ikimashita. _____

_____

4. Kore wa tabetakatta kudamono desu. _____

_____

5. Noritakatta basu ga ikimashita._____

_____

6. Kyō watashi wa kinō tabetakunakatta kudamono o tabemasu.

_____

Translate into rōmaji:

7. At this shop, there isn't a thing that I want to buy. _____

_____

8. I don't do things that I don't want to do._____

_____

9. Yesterday, I saw the movie that I wanted to see._____

_____

10. This is the book that I wanted to read. _____

_____

11. My elder brother went to a party to which he did not want to

go. _____

12. Right now (from now), I am going to read the book that I did

not want to read yesterday._____

_____

Japanese Adjectives Have Tenses

You know that every adjective can be written as an adjective clause. The adjective *big* of *I eat a big apple* may be replaced by an adjective clause to form *I eat an apple that is big*.

For *i*-adjectives, form past and negative past adjectives by changing *_i* with *_katta* and *_ku nakatta*, respectively.

omoshiroi hon	the book that is interesting (the interesting book)
omoshiroku nai hon	the book that is not interesting (the uninteresting book)
omoshirokatta hon	the book that was interesting
omoshiroku nakatta hon	the book that was not interesting

Ano omoshirokatta hito wa Tarō-kun no ojīsan desu.
That person who was interesting is Taro's grandfather.

Watashi wa kono karēraisu o kinō no oishiku nakatta niku de tsukurimashita.
I made this Indian curry with yesterday's meat, which was not delicious.

Tense of Na-Adjectives

For *na*-adjectives, you may obtain past and negative past adjectives by replacing *na* with *datta* and *de (wa) nakatta* respectively.

suki na hito	the person (somebody) likes
suki de (wa) nai hito	the person (somebody) does not like
suki datta hito	the person (somebody) liked
suki de (wa) nakatta hito	the person (somebody) did not like

Ima boku wa mukashi kirai datta Nihon ga suki desu.
Now I like Japan, which I disliked a long time ago.

Mukashi kirei de nakatta Hanako-san wa ima kirei ni nari-mashita.
Hanako, who was not pretty a long time ago, has become pretty now.

Complete the adjective table below.

Meaning	Present	Negative Present	Past	Negative Past
big	ōkii	ōkiku nai	ōkikatta	ōkiku nakatta
	akai			
	isogashii			
	genki na			
	benri na			
	suki na	suki de (wa) nai	suki datta	suki de (wa) nakatta

Exercise 4

Translate into English:

1. Otōto wa karai karēraisu ga kirai desu. _____

_____

2. Kinō watashi-tachi wa omoshiroku nai eiga o gakkō de

mimashita. _____

3. Hon-ya ni hoshikatta hon ga arimasen deshita. _____

_____

4. Watashi wa tanoshiku nakatta toki no koto o kakimashita.

_____

Exercise 5

▶

5. Watashi wa rippa na isha ni naritai desu.

_____

6. Benri de nai apāto wa yasui desu.

_____

7. Shinsetsu datta hito wa Hanako-san no onēsan deshita.

_____

8. Hanako-san wa mukashi jōzu de nakatta tenisu ga totemo

jōzu ni narimashita. _____

_____

Translate into rōmaji:

9. The long holiday has finished. _____

_____

10. Let's go to the place that is not dangerous. _____

_____

11. That isn't the dog that was noisy. _____

_____

12. I bought the dress that was not too expensive. _____

_____

13. I did a stupid thing yesterday. _____

_____

14. We took (our) residence at a not very convenient place

(**sumimasu**—to live, reside, take up residence). _____

_____

15. The person whom I liked got married. _____

_____

Let's Read Japanese: Hiragana

Although you have already learned all the sentence structures there are to learn in this book, remember that Japanese is not written in romanized characters. Romanized characters (**rōmaji**) are used to represent the sounds of Japanese in a way that makes it easy for you to read, although Japanese is written in completely different characters.

There are four different types of characters in Japanese. They are **hiragana**, **katakana**, **kanji** and **rōmaji** . The word **watashi**, *I*, may be written in these four ways as shown below (although you would not normally write **watashi** in katakana).

わたし	ワタシ	私	watashi
Hiragana	**Katakana**	**Kanji**	**Rōmaji**

Japanese sentences are written in combinations of **hiragana**, **katakana** and **kanji**.

In this lesson, you will learn the differences among **hiragana**, **katakana**, **kanji** and **rōmaji** so that you will be able to use them correctly. You will also learn to read sentences in **hiragana**.

Differences among Hiragana, Katakana, Kanji and Rōmaji

Hiragana consists of phonetic symbols representing sounds (syllables) with no individual meanings. There are forty-six different symbols in **hiragana**, and you can write entire sentences with **hiragana** alone.
Katakana consists of phonetic symbols representing sounds (syllables), just like **hiragana**. For every **hiragana** symbol, there is a **katakana** symbol. The difference between **hiragana** and **katakana** is that **katakana** is used mostly for foreign

words (other than Chinese), for which no Japanese words existed, and which became Japanese words after going through some phonetic transformations.

For example, television became テレビ (**terebi**) in Japanese.

Katakana characters are the simplest of all the characters. Each character resembles a combination of a few straight and curved lines in different directions and at different angles.

Kanji consists of characters introduced from China many years ago. They were derived from pictographs (pictures) and ideograms (symbols used to represent ideas), and each character represents a complete word or meaning. **Kanji** characters are the most complicated of all the characters, and they look like pictures for obvious reasons.

木 (ki) tree

人 (hito) person

There are more than 50,000 **kanji** in existence, but only about 1,800 of them are used commonly. Japanese school children spend a great amount of time learning **kanji** characters at schools. The level of one's education is reflected in the number of **kanji** characters one uses in one's writing: the more **kanji** one uses, the more educated one appears to be.

Rōmaji characters are combinations of the English alphabet. They represent the Japanese sounds, just as **hiragana** and **katakana** do, but in the English alphabet to help English speakers learn Japanese pronunciation. Although they are taught in schools, they are not customarily used in Japanese writing. Lately, **rōmaji** has become indispensable for using a Japanese word processor: you type sentences in **rōmaji**, and the word processor converts them into **hiragana**, **katakana** or **kanji** accordingly. This is due to the fact that there are just too many different characters in Japanese, and a computer keyboard cannot have that many keys.

Writing in Japanese

When you write a Japanese sentence, you may write it entirely in *hiragana*. If you do know *kanji* for any word, you should use it, and if a word is an imported word, write it in *katakana*.

The sentences below are perceived as being written by an educated person.

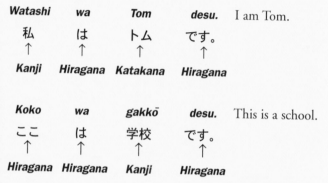

Watashi	wa	Tom	desu.	I am Tom.
私	は	トム	です。	
↑	↑	↑	↑	
Kanji	Hiragana	Katakana	Hiragana	

Koko	wa	gakkō	desu.	This is a school.
ここ	は	学校	です。	
↑	↑	↑	↑	
Hiragana	Hiragana	Kanji	Hiragana	

The sentences below are perceived as being written by a less educated person.

Watashiwa	Tom	desu.	I am Tom.
わたしは	とむ	です。	
↑	↑	↑	↑	

All the characters are in *hiragana*.

Koko	wa	gakkō	desu.	This is a school.
ここ	は	がっこう	です。	
↑	↑	↑	↑	

All the characters are in *hiragana*.

Syllables in Hiragana

The table shows the **hiragana** for each **rōmaji** syllable.

Vowels

a	あ	i	い	u	う	e	え	o	お

Basic syllables

ka	か	ki	き	ku	く	ke	け	ko	こ
sa	さ	shi	し	su	す	se	せ	so	そ
ta	た	chi	ち	tsu	つ	te	て	to	と
na	な	ni	に	nu	ぬ	ne	ね	no	の
ha	は	hi	ひ	fu	ふ	he	へ	ho	ほ
ma	ま	mi	み	mu	む	me	め	mo	も
ya	や			yu	ゆ			yo	よ
ra	ら	ri	り	ru	る	re	れ	ro	ろ
wa	わ							wo	を
n	ん								

Second third: Modified syllables

ga	が	gi	ぎ	gu	ぐ	ge	げ	go	ご
za	ざ	ji	じ	zu	ず	ze	ぜ	zo	ぞ
da	だ	ji	ぢ	zu	づ	de	で	do	ど
ba	ば	bi	び	bu	ぶ	be	べ	bo	ぼ
pa	ぱ	pi	ぴ	pu	ぷ	pe	ぺ	po	ぽ

Third third: *Ya, Yu, Yo* syllables

kya	きゃ	kyu	きゅ	kyo	きょ
sha	しゃ	shu	しゅ	sho	しょ
cha	ちゃ	chu	ちゅ	cho	ちょ
nya	にゃ	nyu	にゅ	nyo	にょ

▶

hya	ひゃ	hyu	ひゅ	hyo	ひょ
mya	みゃ	myu	みゅ	myo	みょ
rya	りゃ	ryu	りゅ	ryo	りょ
gya	ぎゃ	gyu	ぎゅ	gyo	ぎょ
ja	じゃ	ju	じゅ	jo	じょ
bya	びゃ	byu	びゅ	byo	びょ
pya	ぴゃ	pyu	ぴゅ	pyo	ぴょ

Remember that both **rōmaji** and **hiragana** are phonetic symbols (associated with speech sounds) and that a syllable in **hiragana** may be represented by a syllable in **rōmaji**.

わ	↔	wa
た	↔	ta
わたし	↔	watashi

Modified Syllables and Ya, Yu, Yo

The **hiragana** in the second third, called modified syllables, are obtained by adding " ゛" or " ゜" to each character in rows 2, 3, 4 and 6. Note that there are two different hiragana for **ji** and for **zu**: both じ and ち are pronounced as **ji**, and both ず and づ are pronounced as **zu**.

The third third contains contracted syllables (or **Ya, Yu, Yo** syllables), because two syllables are contracted to obtain a single syllable. Consider the syllable **kya**. When you pronounce **kya**, the syllable starts out as **ki** and ends with **ya**. When the two syllables are pronounced as one syllable, you hear **kya**. When it is written in **hiragana**, the first letter remains the same but the second letter is written smaller.

き	ki	+	や	ya	→	きゃ	kya
み	mi	+	よ	yo	→	みょ	myo
き	ki	+	ゆ	yu	→	きゅ	kyu

Small Characters

Whether a character is small or standard size makes a great difference to its meaning. For example, いしや *ishiya,* means *a stonemason* while いしゃ *isha,* means *a medical doctor*. You can see that no such confusion arises when they are written in rōmaji. The small characters や, ゅ, ょ (and っ) are placed at the bottom lefthand corner of the area that a normal-size character would take up, when Japanese is written horizontally; and at the top righthand corner of that area, when Japanese is written vertically.

Here is the word *isha*, *medical doctor* in hiragana, written horizontally, and vertically.

いしゃ   い
                し
                ゃ

Write the following hiragana words in rōmaji, using the table that begins on page 260 if necesary, and then translate them into English.

1. こんにちわ _____

2. ただいま _____

3. すみません _____

4. みかん _____

5. りんご _____

6. やさい _____

7. くだもの _____

8. せんせい _____

9. いぬ _____

🔊 You will hear a word in Japanese; write it below in hiragana.

1.＿＿＿＿＿＿＿＿＿＿   6. ＿＿＿＿＿＿＿＿＿＿＿＿

2.＿＿＿＿＿＿＿＿＿＿   7. ＿＿＿＿＿＿＿＿＿＿＿＿

3.＿＿＿＿＿＿＿＿＿＿   8. ＿＿＿＿＿＿＿＿＿＿＿＿

4.＿＿＿＿＿＿＿＿＿＿   9. ＿＿＿＿＿＿＿＿＿＿＿＿

5.＿＿＿＿＿＿＿＿＿＿   10. ＿＿＿＿＿＿＿＿＿＿＿

Long Vowels and Double Consonants

Converting *rōmaji* into *hiragana*, and vice versa, is fairly straightforward, except when the words include long vowels or double consonants. Here are the rules for converting long vowels and double consonants.

Long Vowels

Look at the romanized syllables in the hiragana table.

a appears in the first column in **a, ka, sa, ta, na,** etc. Hence the long vowel **ā** may occur in **ā, kā, sā, tā, nā,** etc. These are pronounced as **a/a, ka/a, sa/a, ta/a, na/a,** and they are written as ああ, かあ, さあ, たあ, なあ, in hiragana. For example, **okāsan** is written as おかあさん.

Look at *i* in the hiragana table.

i appears in the second column in **i, ki, shi, chi, ni,** etc. Hence the long vowel **ī** may occur in **ī, kī, shī, chī, nī,** etc. These are pronounced as **i/i, ki/i, shi/i, chi/i, ni/i,** and they are written as いい, きい, しい, ちい, にい. For example, **onīsan** is written as おにいさん.

▶

The long vowel *ū* occurs in the third column in *ū*, *kū*, *sū*, *tsū*, *nū*, etc.

These are pronounced as *u/u*, *ku/u*, *su/u*, *tsu/u*, etc., and they are written as うう, くう, すう, つう, etc. For example, *senpūki* is written as せんぷうき.

The long vowel *ē* may occur in the fourth column in *ē*, *kē*, *sē*, *tē*, *nē*, etc.

These are pronounced as *e/e*, *ke/e*, *se/e*, *te/e*, *ne/e*, etc., and written as えい, けい, せい, てい, ねい, etc. An exception to this rule is *onēsan*, which is written as おね<u>え</u>さん. Most often *ē* occurs in words written in *katakana*.

The long vowel *ō* may occur in the fifth column in *ō*, *kō*, *sō*, *tō*, *nō*, etc.

These are pronounced as *o/o*, *ko/o*, *so/o*, *to/o*, *no/o*, etc., and written as おう, こう, そう, とう, のう. *Otōsan* is written as おとうさん. There are some exceptions to this rule. The most important, and the only one encountered in this book, is that of *ōkii*, which is written as お<u>お</u>きい.

obāsan	おば<u>あ</u>さん	*arigatō*	ありがと<u>う</u>
ojīsan	おじ<u>い</u>さん	*dōzo*	ど<u>う</u>ぞ
yūbinkyoku	ゆ<u>う</u>びんきょく	*Tōkyō*	と<u>う</u>きょ<u>う</u>
otōto	おと<u>う</u>と		

In summary い and う each have two different pronunciations.

- い is pronounced as *i* except for some long vowels, in which it is pronounced as *e*.
- う is pronounced as *u* except for some long vowels, in which it is pronounced as *o*.

When you see い or う, the only way to correctly pronounce it is to know the pronunciation of the word which contains it.

Double Consonants (kk, pp, tt, ss)

A word with a double consonant in **rōmaji** is written in
hiragana by replacing the "(small pause)" with a small っ.
Nippon is pronounced as **Ni**/(small pause)**/po/n,** and written as にっぽん.
Similarly, **kitte, kippu** and **zasshi** are written as きって,
きっぷ and ざっし.

Write the pronunciations a, i, u, e or o for the following
underlined hiragana.

Exercise 3

1. う<u>し</u>	cow	<u>u</u>
2. ど<u>う</u>ぞ	Please	_____
3. おか<u>あ</u>さん	mother	_____
4. こ<u>う</u>えん	park	_____
5. よ<u>う</u>ちえん	kindergarten	_____
6. ありが<u>と</u><u>う</u>	Thank you	_____
7. おは<u>よ</u><u>う</u>ございます	Good morning	_____
8. <u>お</u>かえりなさい	Welcome home	_____
9. ゆ<u>う</u>びんきょく	post office	_____
10. いも<u>う</u>と	younger sister	_____

265

Exercise 4

🔘 You will hear a word in Japanese; write it below in hiragana.

1._____ 6._____

2._____ 7._____

3._____ 8._____

4._____ 9._____

5._____ 10._____

How to Read Japanese Sentences

There are no capital letters in Japanese. The small や,
ゆ, よ and つ are written about a quarter of the size of
the other characters. There is no question mark used in
Japanese because the particle **ka,** at the end of a sentence,
indicates that it is a question. The end of a sentence is
denoted by " 。" (period).

When the sounds **wa, e** and **o** are particles, they must be
written as は, へ and を.

Watashi _wa_ Hanako desu. The first **wa** is a part of a word,
and so it is written as わ. The second **wa** is a particle, and
so it is written as は.

Watashi wa _eki e_ ikimasu. The first **e** is a part of a word,
and so it is written as え. The second **e** is a particle, and so
it is written as へ.

Otōsan wa ringo _o_ tabemasu. The first **o** is a part of a
word, and so it is written as お. The second **o** is a particle,
and so it is written as を.

Japanese sentences are traditionally written without
spaces between words. Punctuation marks, "、", which are
comparable to English commas, are inserted as in English.

Although there are no spaces between words in written Japanese, in this book we will insert a small space after each adverb,adjective and particle to make learning easier. If there is more than one particle, one after another, a small space will be inserted after the second particle.This is a common practice used to avoid confusion when Japanese children are taught to read and write.

Japanese sentences are written either horizontally or vertically. Books on mathematics, science, music and foreign languages are usually written horizontally to accommodate Arabic numerals, scientific symbols, musical notes and foreign languages.

Novels, and other books that contain only words, are written vertically. To do this, you proceed from top to bottom and from right to left. The periods " 。" and punctuation marks ", " are both placed at the same location as small characters, that is, at the top right half of the square when the sentence is written vertically, and at the bottom left half of the square when the sentence is written horizontally.

Here is the Japanese phrase

Kore wa nihon no kitte de wa arimasen.

written both horizontally and vertically.

で	こ
は	れ
	は
あ	に
り	ほ
ま	ん
せ	の
ん	
。	
	き
	っ
	て

こ	れ	は		に	ほ	ん	の		き	っ	て
で	は		あ	り	ま	せ	ん	。			

Exercise 5

Convert the following sentences into rōmaji and then translate them into English.

1. ここは　えきです。 _____

_____

_____

2. これは　わたしの　いぬです。 _____

_____

_____

3. あなたは　すしを　たべますか。 _____

_____

_____

4. あした、　わたしたちは　やまへ　いきます。 _____

_____

5. これから、　あなたは　なにを　しますか。 _____

_____

_____

6. あそこに　くだものやが　あります。 _____

_____

_____

7. わたしは　はなこです。 _____

_____

_____

Why Japanese is Written With Kanji, Hiragana and Katakana

In the beginning, Japanese was a spoken language only. In the fifth century, the Chinese method of writing was introduced to Japan. Since the Chinese and Japanese languages are completely different (Chinese does not have particles and has a different word order from Japanese), people devised many systems over the years, but one particular system that became prominent is called **Manyōgana**; the Japanese syllable was written using the Chinese character of the same sound. Japanese sentences written in this way were all in Chinese characters, but were incomprehensible to a Chinese person. About 1,000 Chinese characters were used to represent about 100 Japanese syllables, and this became the basis for the future development of **hiragana** and **katakana**. In the mid-ninth century, **hiragana** developed from **Manyōgana** to represent Japanese sounds. In those days, people used brushes and ink to write Chinese characters, which have many strokes. There were three different styles of writing Chinese characters. One was to write characters rigidly (see "a" in the diagram on the next page), another was the cursive style in which one rarely lifts the brush off the paper, and the third style is something in between ("b"). From the cursive style of writing, **hiragana** was created.

(a)   (b)   (c)

The Chinese script 女, written in three different styles:
(a) **kaisho** (non-cursive style); (b) **gyōsho** (semi-cursive style);
(c) **sōsho** (cursive style)

Imported Words: Katakana

Katakana is used in the following situations:

1. Words of foreign origin, other than Chinese, which have become Japanese. Foreign words which did not exist in Japanese were modified to fit into the Japanese phonetic system, and written in *katakana*.

   Banana became *banana* バナナ.
   Radio became *rajio* ラジオ.
   Baseball became *bēsubōru* ベースボール.

2. Foreign personal names, places and other proper nouns. These are written as closely as possible to the way they are pronounced.

   Smith is *Sumisu* スミス.
   Ann is *An* アン.
   America is *Amerika* アメリカ.

3. Describing the sounds around us, like the purring of a cat or barking of a dog.

   Wanwan ワンワン for woof woof.
   Nyā ニャー for meow.

Syllables in Katakana

On the next page is the table of *katakana*. Unlike *hiragana*, which is made up of cursive lines, *katakana* is made up of simpler straight and curved lines.

▶

Vowels

a ア		*i* イ		*u* ウ		*e* エ		*o* オ	

First third

ka カ	*ki* キ	*ku* ク	*ke* ケ	*ko* コ
sa サ	*shi* シ	*su* ス	*se* セ	*so* ソ
ta タ	*chi* チ	*tsu* ツ	*te* テ	*to* ト
na ナ	*ni* ニ	*nu* ヌ	*ne* ネ	*no* ノ
ha ハ	*hi* ヒ	*fu* フ	*he* ヘ	*ho* ホ
ma マ	*mi* ミ	*mu* ム	*me* メ	*mo* モ
ya ヤ		*yu* ユ		*yo* ヨ
ra ラ	*ri* リ	*ru* ル	*re* レ	*ro* ロ
wa ワ				*wo* ヲ
n ン				

Second third: Modified syllables

ga ガ	*gi* ギ	*gu* グ	*ge* ゲ	*go* ゴ
za ザ	*ji* ジ	*zu* ズ	*ze* ゼ	*zo* ゾ
da ダ	*ji* ヂ	*zu* ヅ	*de* デ	*do* ド
ba バ	*bi* ビ	*bu* ブ	*be* ベ	*bo* ボ
pa パ	*pi* ピ	*pu* プ	*pe* ペ	*po* ポ

Third third: Ya, Yu, Yo, syllables

kya キャ	*kyu* キュ	*kyo* キョ
sha シャ	*shu* シュ	*sho* ショ
cha チャ	*chu* チュ	*cho* チョ
nya ニャ	*nyu* ニュ	*nyo* ニョ
hya ヒャ	*hyu* ヒュ	*hyo* ヒョ
mya ミャ	*myu* ミュ	*myo* ミョ
rya リャ	*ryu* リュ	*ryo* リョ
gya ギャ	*gyu* ギュ	*gyo* ギョ
ja ジャ	*ju* ジュ	*jo* ジョ
bya ビャ	*byu* ビュ	*byo* ビョ
pya ピャ	*pyu* ピュ	*pyo* ピョ

Hiragana and Katakana: Similarities

Just like in **hiragana**, modified syllables in **katakana** are formed by adding "ﾞ" or "ﾟ" to characters in rows 2, 3, 4, and 6. **Ya**, **yu** and **yo** syllables are formed by adding ャ, ュ and ョ.

1. When **hiragana** has "ﾞ" or "ﾟ," so does **katakana**.

hiragana	katakana
ga (が) is **ka** (か) + "ﾞ."	**ga** (ガ) is **ka** (カ) + "ﾞ."
pa (ぱ) is **ha** (は) + "ﾟ."	**pa** (パ) is **ha** (ハ) + "ﾟ."

2. When **hiragana** is followed by a small ゃ, ゅ or ょ, so is **katakana**.

hiragana	katakana
kya (きゃ) is **ki** (き) + **ya** (ゃ)	**kya** (キャ) is **ki** (キ) + **ya** (ャ)
gyu (ぎゅ) is **gi** (ぎ) + **yu** (ゅ)	**gyu** (ギュ) is **gi** (ギ) + **yu** (ュ)

Since **katakana** symbols are syllabic, one syllable in **katakana** may be represented by one syllable in **rōmaji**, just as in **hiragana**.

te ↔ テ   **su** ↔ ス   **tesuto** ↔ テスト

Some words are written in a combination of **katakana** and **hiragana**. **Amerika-jin** literally means *America-person,* hence **Amerika** is written in **katakana** and **jin** is written in **hiragana**: アメリカじん.

Exercise 1

🔘 You will hear a word in Japanese; write it below in katakana.

1. _____   6. _____

2. _____   7. _____

3. _____   8. _____

4. _____   9. _____

5. _____   10. _____

Convert the following katakana into rōmaji and then translate
them into English.

Exercise 2

1. オレンジ _____

_____

2. トイレ _____

_____

3. ラジオ _____

_____

4. バナナ _____

_____

5. ペン _____

_____

6. プレゼント _____

_____

Long Vowels and Double Consonants in Katakana

When converting **rōmaji** words into **katakana**, all long
vowels are indicated by using horizontal lines " — ," when
you write horizontally.

bōru ボ ー ル
kōhī コ ー ヒ ー
uētā ウ エ ー タ ー

When writing **katakana** vertically, a vertical line " | " is used
for long vowels.

```
ウ      コ      ボ
エ      |       ー
ー      ヒ      ル
タ      |
|
```

▶

273

Double Consonants

For double consonants, the same rule applies as in *hiragana*:
"(short pause)" is replaced by small ッ.

koppu is pronounced as *ko*/(short pause)/*pu* and written as
コップ.

Exercise 3

🔊 You will hear a word in Japanese; write it below in katakana.

1._____   6._____

2._____   7._____

3._____   8._____

4._____   9._____

5._____   10._____

Exercise 4

Translate the following sentences into rōmaji and English.

1. わたしの　おかあさんは　アメリカじんです。

_____

_____

2. おとうさんは　ラジオを　にわで　ききます。

_____

_____

3. まことくんは　テレビを　みません。

_____

_____

4. スミスさんは　コーヒーを　のみます。

_____

_____

5. わたしたちは　ステーキを　たべました。

_____

_____

6. トイレは　どこですか。

_____

_____

Japanized English Words Japanese contains many Japanized English words, some of which you can recognize easily, such as **aisukurīmu**, *ice cream*; **conpūtā**, *computer* and **banana**, *banana*. However, there are far more Japanized English words that you will probably not recognize. There are patterns of Japanized English words as follows.

1. New words formed from sets of English words: **wan-man-basu**, *one-man-bus*, meaning a bus in which the driver, not the conductor, collects the fares.
2. New words from the first two or three syllables of English words: **apāto**, *apart*ment; **nega**, *nega*tive (of a film); **biru**, *buil*ding; **infure**, *infl*ation.
3. New words from initials: **ōeru** meaning *o*ffice *l*ady.
4. New words from abbreviating compound words: for example, **wāpuro**, *wor*d *pro*cessor.
5. New words from combining Japanese and English words: for example, Japanese word **ha**, *tooth*, combined with Japanized English word **burasshi**, *brush*, creates **haburashi**, *toothbrush*.

275

Kanji

How Pictures Became Characters

Kanji, which originated between 4,000 and 5,000 years ago in China, were originally simple pictures of objects in daily life. These illustrations show you some transformations of objects (sun, moon, mountain) into words.

With time, pictographic words alone could not express everything people needed to. These illustrations show you how some abstract ideas (above, below and middle), were transformed into words.

above

below

middle

More Kanji

More complicated **kanji** characters, composed of combinations of simple **kanji** characters, were developed with time.

木＋木 → 林 *wood* (few trees make a wood)
木＋木＋木 → 森 *forest* (many trees make a forest)
日＋月 → 明 *bright* (sun and moon together make
                                things very bright)

As the writing system developed, characters were needed to express even more complicated words, and two or more **kanji** characters were combined to make one word.

The characters 山 *mountain* and 林 *wood* were combined to make the word related to both: 山林 **sanrin** *wood in the mountain (forest on a mountain)*

Pronouncing Kanji

Each **kanji** character may be pronounced in more than one way depending on the other **kanji** character(s) it is combined with to make another word. So, when you are learning to pronounce **kanji**, you must remember the whole word (a combination of one or more characters) and not just one particular character, as may be seen in the examples below.

日 and 山 have several different pronunciations, shown below (the pronunciations of 日 and 山 are underlined).

Since the character 日 was derived from *sun*, it was combined with other **kanji** characters to make words related to either *sun* or *day*.

日   *hi*   sun, daytime, day

月曜日	**getsuyōbi** *	Monday
六日	**muika**	sixth day of a month, six days
元日	**ganjitsu**	first day of a year
一日	**ichi-nichi**	one day

Since the character 山 was derived from *mountain*, it was used to make words related to *mountain*.

山	**yama**	mountain
山林	**sanrin**	wood in the mountain
火山	**kazan**	volcano (fire and mountain makes volcano)

*__bi__ is the phonetic transformation of hi.

Numbers

Although prices in train stations, supermarkets, department stores, etc. are listed horizontally in Arabic numerals, many restaurants, especially the traditional ones, list prices vertically in **kanji**.

〇	**zero**	0
一	**ichi**	1
二	**ni**	2
三	**san**	3
四	**yon/shi**	4
五	**go**	5
六	**roku**	6
七	**nana/shichi**	7
八	**hachi**	8
九	**kyū /ku**	9
十	**jū**	10
百	**hyaku**	100
千	**sen**	1,000
萬	**man**	10,000

Japanese Money

The first Japanese characters you really must understand
are those written on Japanese money: you don't want to pay
¥20,000 for your taxi fare instead of ¥2,000. You may
notice in the characters below that ¥ stands for *yen*, just as
$ stands for *dollar*, and 円-*en* at the end of each Japanese
currency refers to *yen*.

一万円	*ichi-man-en*	¥10,000
五千円	*go-sen-en*	¥5,000
千円	*sen-en*	¥1,000
五百	*go-hyaku-en*	¥500
百円	*hyaku-en*	¥100
五十円	*go-jū-en*	¥50
五円	*go-en*	¥5
一円	*ichi-en*	¥1

Public Transportation

At international airports and major train stations, most
signs will be in both Japanese and English. However, if you
end up in a local train station or a small town, you will need
to recognize the following signs.

案内所	*annaisho*	Information
荷物一時預り所	*nimotsu-ichiji-azukarisho*	Luggage Check-in
コインロッカー	*koin-rokkā*	Coin Lockers
精算所	*seisansho*	Fare Adjustment
きっぷうりば	*kippu-uriba*	Ticket Office
新幹線のりば	*Shinkansen-noriba*	Shinkansen Tracks
JR線のりば	*JR-sen-noriba*	JR Line Tracks
電話	*denwa*	Telephone
国際電話	*kokusai-denwa*	International Telephone

自動きっぷうりば	*jidō-kippu-uriba*	Automatic Ticket Dispenser (Machines)
お手洗	*otearai*	Washrooms
みどりの窓口	*midori-no-madoguchi**	Train Reservation Office (for Shinkansen tickets)

Other Transportation

バス	*basu*	bus
タクシー	*takushī*	taxi
バスの停留所	*basu no teiryūjo*	bus stop
地下鉄	*chikatetsu*	underground, subway

Exercise 1

Imagine yourself in Japan. From the options given below, choose the signs you must follow to get to the following places:

1. You want to buy a train ticket. _____

2. You want to go to a washroom. _____

3. You want to take a bus. _____

4. You want to take a taxi. _____

5. You want to check your luggage. _____

6. You want to make a phone call. _____

7. You want to reserve a seat on a Shinkansen. _____

8. You want to get on the Shinkansen. _____

a. ↑ お手洗   **b.** ← タクシー
c. 新幹線のりば →   **d.** きっぷうりば →
e. 荷物一時預り所 →   **f.** ← みどりの窓口
g. ← バス   **h.** ↑ 電話

Answer Key

Exercise 1: **1.** mo **2.** ri **3.** te **4.** ku **5.** su **6.** na **7.** hi **8.** ya **9.** no **10.** ga **11.** bi **12.** kyu **13.** sha **14.** cho **15.** a **16.** ā **17.** o **18.** ō **19.** i **20.** ī
Exercise 2: **1.** o-ya-su-mi-na-sa-i **2.** ta-da-i-ma **3.** ko-n-ba-n-wa
Exercise 3: **1.** a **2.** d **3.** h **4.** c **5.** f **6.** i **7.** e **8.** g **9.** b
Exercise 4: **1.** ha/ji/me/ma/shi/te **2.** o/ka/e/ri/na/sa/i **3.** ko/n/ni/chi/wa **4.** su/mi/ma/se/n **5.** o/to/o/sa/n **6.** o/ka/a/sa/n **7.** ko/(small pause)/pu **8.** ki/(small pause)/te

Exercise 1: **1.** Okaerinasai **2.** Hajimemashite **3.** Konnichiwa **4.** Konbanwa **5.** Ohayōgozaimasu **6.** Sayōnara **7.** Dō itashimashite **8.** Oyasuminasai
Exercise 2: **1.** d **2.** b **3.** c **4.** e **5.** a **6.** h **7.** g **8.** f

Exercise 1: **1.** d **2.** h **3.** a **4.** g **5.** f **6.** e **7.** b **8.** c
Exercise 2: **1.** May I have a banana please? **2.** May I have sushi please? **3.** steak and bread **4.** May I have steak and bread please? **5.** a coffee or a juice **6.** May I have a coffee or a juice please? **7.** May I have an apple, a tangerine or a banana please? **8.** Ringo o kudasai. **9.** Karēraisu o kudasai. **10.** banana ka orenj **11.** Banana ka orenji o kudasai. **12.** tenpura to soba **13.** Tenpura to soba o kudasai. **14.** Kōhī to pan to tonkatsu o kudasai.
Exercise 3: **1.** Banana o kudasai. **2.** Jūsu o kudasai. **3.** Sarada o kudasai. **4.** Sutēki o kudasai. **5.** Kōhī to sandoicchi o kudasai.

Exercise 1: **1.** Nihon-jin, gakusei **2.** Tom, Amerika-jin, gakusei
Exercise 2: **1.** sensei **2.** kun **3.** chan **4.** sensei
Exercise 3: **1.** are **2.** sore **3.** kore
Exercise 4: **1.** father **2.** mother **3.** Ken
Exercise 5: **1.** kaishain **2.** okāsan, sensei **3.** okāsan, Kanada-jin **4.** Tom, Ken **5.** onīsan
Exercise 6: **1.** lion, tiger **2.** bear **3.** giraffe, elephant
Exercise 7: **1.** kore **2.** koko **3.** sore **4.** soko **5.** are **6.** asoko
Exercise 8: **1.** I am Hanako. **2.** This is Amy. **3.** This is a cat. **4.** Those (over there) are (my) younger sister and (my) younger brother. **5.** That (over there) is (our) teacher. **6.** Watashi wa Betty desu. **7.** Watashi-tachi wa gakusei desu. **8.** Kore wa okā san desu. **9.** Kore wa buta to ushi desu.

10. Betty wa imōto desu.

Exercise 9: **1.** Kore wa imōto desu. **2.** Sore wa onēsan desu. **3.** Are wa otōsan desu. **4.** Kore wa neko desu. **5.** Are wa tori desu. **6.** Koko wa ginkō desu. **7.** Asoko wa yama desu.

Lesson 5

Exercise 1: **1.** Kore wa usagi desu ka. Is this a rabbit? **2.** Anata wa (o)isha-san desu ka. Are you a medical doctor? **3.** Koko wa ima desu ka. Is this a family room? **4.** Asoko wa byōin desu ka. Is that (place far away) a hospital? **5.** Sore wa suika desu ka. Is that a watermelon?

Exercise 2: **1.** Kore wa usagi de wa arimasen. **2.** Anata wa (o)isha-san de wa arimasen. **3.** Koko wa ima de wa arimasen. **4.** Asoko wa byōin de wa arimasen. **5.** Sore wa suika de wa arimasen.

Exercise 3: **1.** Excuse me. Is this (place) a post-office? No, this (place) is not a post office. This (place) is a bank. **2.** Is Tom French? No, Tom is not French. Tom is American. **3.** Anata wa Amy-san desu ka. Iie watashi wa Amy-san de wa arimasen. Watashi wa Betty desu. **4.** Anata wa Amerika-jin desu ka. Iie watashi wa Amerika-jin de wa arimasen. Watashi wa Doitsu-jin desu. **5.** Koko wa ginkō desu ka. Hai sō desu.

Exercise 4: **1.** Iie kore wa onēsan de wa arimasen.　Kore wa obāsan desu. **2.** Iie kore wa jagaimo de wa arimasen.　Kore wa ninjin desu. **3.** Iie koko wa gakkō de wa arimasen.　Koko wa kōen desu.

Exercise 5: **1.** (a) obāsan (b) obāsan (c) dare **2.** (a) ninjin (b) ninjin (c) nan **3.** (a) kōen (b) kōen (c) doko

Exercise 6: **1.** Anata wa Imaeda Kazuko-san/sensei desu. **2.** Hai anata wa sensei desu. **3.** Iie anata wa Amerika-jin de wa arimasen **4.** Hai anata wa otona desu.

Exercise 7: **1.** Kore wa nan desu ka. **2.** Sore wa nan desu ka. **3.** Are wa nan desu ka. **4.** Kore wa dare desu ka. **5.** Sore wa dare desu ka. **6.** Are wa dare desu ka. **7.** Koko wa doko desu ka. **8.** Soko wa doko desu ka. **9.** Asoko wa doko desu ka.

Exercise 8: **1.** What is that (over there)? That is a book. **2.** Where is this (place)? This (place) is a park. **3.** What is that? This is sushi. **4.** Where is the house? **5.** Are wa dare desu ka. Are wa sensei desu. **6.** Kore wa nan desu ka. Sore wa hakusai desu. **7.** Koko wa doko desu ka. Koko wa depāto desu. **8.** Anata wa dare desu ka. Watashi wa Peter desu.

Exercise 9: **1.** Purezento wa sakuranbo desu. **2.** Hai onēsan wa gakusei desu. **3.** Mari-san wa imōto desu. **4.** Koko wa kōen desu.

Exercise 1: **1.** watashi no hon **2.** anata no hon **3.** otōto no hon **4.** watashi no otōsan **5.** anata no otōsan **6.** Tom-kun no otōsan

Exercise 2: **2.** Tom's book **3.** (my) younger brother's briefcase **4.** my eye-glasses **5.** your handbag **6.** a friend's umbrella

Exercise 3: **2.** watashi-tachi no tēburu **3.** Tom-kun no kuni **4.** Igirisu no shuto **5.** Eigo no zasshi **6.** tabemono no hon

Exercise 4: **1.** father's **2.** mother's **3.** older brother's **4.** older sister's **5.** mine

Exercise 5: **1.** wa **2.** wa, Is this a school? **3.** wa, no, Is this your school? **4.** wa, to, no, Is this your and your older sister's school? **5.** o, May I have a pen please? **6.** to, o **7.** ka, o

Exercise 6: **1.** doko **2.** dare **3.** nan

Exercise 7: **1.** teacher's chair **2.** mother's purse **3.** Hanako's father **4.** This is my mother. **5.** That is our dog. **6.** Which country is this (place)? This is Italy. **7.** Watashi no tomodachi **8.** Anata no kazoku **9.** Kore wa okāsan no kasa desu. **10.** Watashi no nōto o kudasai. **11.** Watashi wa Eigo no seito desu. **12.** Kore wa nan no kudamono desu ka. Kore wa suika desu.

Exercise 1: **1.** Watashi wa sakana o tabemasu. **2.** Watashi wa miruku o nomimasu. **3.** Watashi wa Eigo o hanashimasu. **4.** Watashi wa shinbun o yomimasu. **5.** Watashi wa okashi o kaimasu. **6.** Watashi wa ongaku o kikimasu. **7.** Watashi wa Nihon-go o naraimasu.

Exercise 2: **1.** Father reads newspapers. **2.** Mother makes bread. **3.** The older brother speaks Japanese. **4.** I eat meat. **5.** The older sister writes a letter. **6.** The younger sister drinks milk. **7.** The younger brother watches TV.

Exercise 3: **1.** nan **2.** nani, What language do you speak? **3.** nani, What do you drink?

Exercise 4: **1.** I watch TV. **2.** I and my younger brother learn Japanese. **3.** My father reads newspapers and magazines. **4.** We listen to the music. **5.** Do you speak Japanese? **6.** What do you eat? **7.** What (kinds of) books do you read? **8.** What do you buy? **9.** What do you make? **10.** Watashi-tachi wa Nihon-go no hon o yomimasu. **11.** Watashi-tachi wa Eigo o naraimasu. **12.** Watashi wa Nihon no ongaku o kikimasu. **13.** Anata no otōsan wa sake o nomimasu ka. **14.** Anata wa nani-go o hanashimasu ka. **15.** Anata wa nani o nomimasu ka. **16.** Anata wa nan no kudamono o tabemasu ka. **17.** Anata wa nan no hon o yomimasu ka. **18.** Anata wa nan no eiga o mimasu ka.

Exercise 1:

Meaning	Positive verb	Negative verb
read	yomimasu	yomimasen
take	torimasu	torimasen
sell	urimasu	urimasen
send	okurimasu	okurimasen
drink	nomimasu	nomimasen

Exercise 2: **1.** Hai nomimasu. **2.** Iie nomimasen. **3.** Iie yomimasen. **4.** Hai naraimasu. **5.** Hai mimasu. **6.** Iie hanashimasen.

Exercise 3: **1.** I do not wash a dog. **2.** (My) older sister does not eat meat. **3.** (My) mother does not buy fruit. **4.** (My) younger sister does not make bread. **5.** (My) younger brother does not read (my) father's books. **6.** I do not speak Japanese. **7.** Do you learn German? No, I don't. **8.** Watashi wa tegami o kakimasen. **9.** Okāsan wa miruku o nomimasen. **10.** Makoto-kun wa udon o tabemasen. **11.** Tom-kun wa shinbun o yomimasen. **12.** Watashi wa ongaku o kikimasen. **13.** Watashi wa Nihon-go o hanashi-masen. **14.** Anata wa kore o kaimasu ka. Iie kaimasen.

Exercise 4: **1.** watch TV **2.** drink wine **3.** buy that **4.** read a magazine **5.** eat steak

Exercise 5: **1.** Nomimasen ka. **2.** Kaimasen ka. **3.** Nihon-go o naraimasen ka. **4.** Yakisoba o tabemasen ka.

Exercise 6: **1.** Would you like to see (watch) this? **2.** Would you like to learn French? **3.** Would you like to listen to the music? **4.** Would you like to speak Japanese? **5.** Would you like to eat sushi? Yes, thank you. **6.** Would you like to drink water? No, thank you. **7.** Eigo o hanashimasen ka. **8.** E o kakimasen ka. **9.** Nihon no ongaku o kikimasen ka. **10.** Doitsu-go o naraimasen ka. **11.** (O)cha o nomimasen ka. Hai itadakimasu.

Exercise 1:

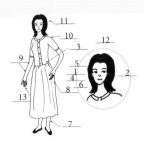

Exercise 2: **1.** Watashi wa tegami o te de kakimasu. **2.** Watashi wa tegami o niwa de kakimasu. **3.** Watashi wa tegami o pen de kakimasu. **4.** Watashi wa tegami o Eigo de kakimasu. **5.** Watashi wa sutēki o daidokoro de tabemasu. **6.** Watashi wa sutēki o naifu to hōku de tabemasu.

Exercise 3: **1.** I eat udon with chopsticks. **2.** (My) older sister listens to the English songs on radio. **3.** With what do you write letters? **4.** (My) father reads books in the room. **5.** We learn English at school. **6.** (My) mother does not make vegetables in the garden. **7.** Where does the grandfather buy bread? **8.** Hanako-san wa neko o mizu de araimasu. **9.** Watashi-tachi wa niku o naifu to hōku de tabemasu. **10.** Obāsan wa hon o megane de yomimasu. **11.** Zō wa banana o hana de tabemasu. **12.** Watashi wa tegami o Nihon-go de kakimasu. **13.** Anata wa ongaku o gakkō de naraimasu ka. **14.** Watashi wa Nihon-go o ie de hanashimasen.

Exercise 4: **1.** What is this in Japanese? **2.** What is this in English?

Exercise 5: **1.** water **2.** leg **3.** cat **4.** inu **5.** hon

Exercise 6: **1.** Ashi wa Eigo de leg desu. **2.** Mimi wa Eigo de ear desu. **3.** Face wa Nihon-go de kao desu. **4.** Mouth wa Nihon-go de kuchi desu.

Exercise 1: **1.** Are wa Hanako-san no onēsan desu ne. **2.** Koko wa (o)tera desu ne. **3.** Mimi wa Eigo de ear desu ne. **4.** Watashi wa kore o tabemasu ne. **5.** Watashi wa inu o araimasu ne.

Exercise 2: **1.** Watashi wa kōhī o tomodachi to nomimasu. **2.** Watashi wa terebi o kazoku to mimasu. **3.** Watashi wa Nihon-go o onīsan to hanashimasu. **4.** Watashi wa Nihon-go o otōto to naraimasu. **5.** Watashi wa ongaku o okāsan to kikimasu.

Exercise 3: **1.** I listen to the music with Makoto. **2.** Would you like to eat sukiyaki with us? **3.** With whom do you speak English? **4.** You are Hanako, aren't you? **5.** That is our bus! **6.** Anata wa nani o Makoto-kun to tsukurimasu ka. **7.** Bideo o watashi to mimasen ka. **8.** Watashi wa Hanako-san to hanashimasen. **9.** Soko wa byōin desu ne. **10.** Kore wa watashi no desu yo.

Exercise 4: **1.** Nihon-go to Eigo o Tom-kun wa hanashimasu yo. **2.** Watashi wa ranchi o Hanako-san to tabemasu, Hanako-san to watashi wa ranchi o tabemasu, Hanako-san to ranchi o watashi wa tabemasu, Ranchi o watashi wa Hanako-san to tabemasu, Ranchi o Hanako-san to watashi wa tabemasu. **3.** none

Exercise 1: ichi, roku, hyaku, ni, nana / shichi, sen, san, hachi, man, yon / shi, kyū/ ku, go, jū

Exercise 2: **2.** 086-255-2100 **3.** 056-362-2561

Exercise 3: **1.** 2,732 **2.** 34,568 **3.** 4,981 **4.** nana-hyaku sanjū go **5.** go-sen ni-hyaku yon-jū ichi **6.** kyū-sen nana-hyaku ni-jū roku

Exercise 4: **1.** 530 **2.** 7,450 **3.** 14,300 **4.** 25,700

Exercise 5: **1.** July 5th **2.** November 10th **3.** March 28th **4.** February 13th
5. October 4th

Exercise 6: **2.** San-gatsu mikka wa Hinamatsuri desu. **3.** Go-gatsu itsuka
wa Kodomo no hi desu. **4.** Shichi-gatsu nanoka wa Tanabata desu. **5.** Jūni-
gatsu nijūgo-nichi wa Kurisumasu desu. **6.** Jūni-gatsu sanjūichi-nichi wa
Ōmisoka desu.

Exercise 7: **1.** Wednesday 5th June 2000. **2.** Monday 25th June 2000.
3. Saturday 2nd March 1981. **4.** Sunday 19th August 172**6. 5.** Ni-sen
yo-nen* ni-gatsu jūyokka doyōbi. (Note that yon-nen has undergone
phonetic transformation and has become yo-nen. Note also that shi is not
used with nen.) **6.** Sen go-hyaku nana-jū kyū/ku-nen jū-gatsu nijūhachi-
nichi sui-yōbi. **7.** Sen yon-hyaku-nen shichi-gatsu itsuka nichi-yōbi.
8. Ni-sen ichi-nen ichi-gatsu tsuitachi getsu-yōbi.

Exercise 1: **1.** 2 o'clock **2.** 4:30 **3.** 4 o' clock **4.** 8:40 **5.** 10:20 **6.** 12 o' clock

Exercise 2: **1.** ni-ji jūgo-fun **2.** yo-ji sanjup-pun **3.** roku-ji **4.** hachi-ji yonjup-pun **5.** jū-ji nijup-pun **6.** jūni-ji

Exercise 3: **1.** 11:25 **2.** 17 minutes to 9 **3.** 6:30 P.M. **4.** 5:30 **5.** gogo ichi-ji
jūgo-fun **6.** gogo jūni-ji sanjup-pun/han **7.** gozen roku-ji yonjūgo-fun
8. gogo shichi-ji nijūsan-pun

Exercise 4: **1.** Ima (wa) hachi-ji nijūgo-fun sugi desu. **2.** Tom-kun wa
kippu o ichi-mai kaimasu. **3.** Kippu wa yon-hyaku hachi-jū-en desu.
4. (O)tsuri wa go-hyaku nijū-en desu. **5.** Densha wa ku-ji go-fun desu.
6. Purattohōmu wa ni-ban sen desu.

Exercise 1: **1.** mo, mo **2.** mo, mo

Exercise 2: **1.** ni **2.** (My) father does not eat dinner at six o' clock. **3.** In the
evening, we watch TV. **4.** In summer, (my) father will sell the house.

Exercise 3: **1.** Shichi-ji han ni Tom-kun wa asa-gohan o tabemasu.
2. Roku-ji ni Tom-kun wa ban-gohan o tabemasu. **3.** Tom-kun wa pan o
asa-gohan ni tabemasu. **4.** Hai mimasu.

Exercise 4: **1.** I drink water. (My) younger sister also drinks water.
2. Both (my) mother and (my) father read books in the room. **3.** Would
you also like to watch a video with us tomorrow? **4.** At night, we write
letters to (our) friends. **5.** The British eat lunch at **1** o'clock. **6.** Hanako-san
wa Furansu-go no hon o yomimasen. Makoto-kun mo Furansu-go no
hon o yomimasen. **7.** Jūni-gatsu ni watashi-tachi wa purezento o ojīsan to
obāsan ni okurimasu. **8.** Watashi wa Eigo mo Nihon-go mo hanashimasu.

9. Otōsan mo okāsan mo Eigo o hanashimasen. **10.** Jūni-ji ni watashi-tachi wa Nihon no ongaku o rajio de kikimasu.

Exercise 5: **1.** Watashi mo tomodachi o ranchi ni manekimasu. **2.** Watashi mo basu o koko de machimasu. **3.** Watashi mo tegami o kōkūbin de okurimasu. **4.** Watashi mo shashin o sensei ni misemasu.

Exercise 6: **1.** I will borrow this. **2.** In spring, the teacher resigns from the school. **3.** In summer, (my) mother will invite (my) grandmother to Japan. **4.** Where does the father stop the car? **5.** Do you wear a hat in winter? **6.** Otōto to watashi wa Robert-kun o (watashi-tachi no) ie ni manekimasu. **7.** Onēsan wa bōshi o atsumemasu. **8.** Watashi wa anata o wasuremasen. **9.** Fuyu anata wa kōto o kimasu ka. **10.** Watashi wa e o otōsan ni mise-masu.

Exercise 1: **1.** Would you like to go to Kyoto next week by train? **2.** Would you like to come to my house for lunch tomorrow? **3.** Would you like to get off the bus here? **4.** Would you like to go out from the station? **5.** Would you like to go to Japanese language class? **6.** Would you like to go to a coffee shop?

Exercise 2: **1.** Otōsan wa kaisha e kisha de ikimasu. **2.** Okāsan wa sūpāmāketto e kuruma de ikimasu. **3.** Iie ikimasen. **4.** Onēsan wa daigaku e ikimasu.

Exercise 3: **1.** Ichi-gatsu kara go-gatsu made otōsan wa gaikoku e ikimasu. From January to May, (my) father will go abroad. **2.** Tōkyō kara Ōsaka made watashi wa kissha de ikimasu. I will go to Tokyo to Osaka by train. **3.** Asa kara yoru made otōto wa terebi o mimasu. From morning to night, (my) younger brother watches TV.

Exercise 4: **1.** In January, Betty will return to America. **2.** Where do you go by train? **3.** (My) older sister also gets off the bus. **4.** Neither (my) younger brother nor I go to school by car. **5.** In spring, (my) grandfather will come to Japan by boat. **6.** Otōsan wa furo kara demasu. **7.** Asa no hachi-ji ni watashi wa gakkō e ikimasu. **8.** Ku-gatsu ni watashi wa Amerika e hikōki de ikimasu. **9.** Natsu Tom-kun wa Amerika e kaerimasen. **10.** Ku-gatsu ni otōto wa yōchien ni* hairimasen. (*ni is used since "entering a kindergar-ten" does not mean a motion of going into a kindergarten, but an event.)

Exercise 1: **1.** Asa hachi-ji ni onēsan wa kao o araimasu. **2.** Hai shimasu. **3.** Hiru onēsan wa (okāsan to) kaimono o shimasu. **4.** Ban onēsan wa deito o shimasu.

Exercise 2: **1.** cook **2.** do not play sumo wrestling **3.** At night, (my) mother knits also. **4.** (My) older brother does not play baseball. **5.** yakusoku o shimasu **6.** tenisu o shimasen **7.** Hachi-gatsu ni watashi-tachi wa ryokō o kuruma de shimasu. **8.** Anata wa nani o gakkō de shimasu ka.

Exercise 3: **2.** torakku o unten shimasu **3.** yasai o ryōri shimasu **4.** Eigo o benkyō shimasu

Exercise 4: **1.** I will cook this. **2.** I will promise that. **3.** Betty does not drive a car. **4.** In August, we will get married (we will marry). **5.** Aki watashi wa Amerika o ryokō shimasu. **6.** Watashi wa sutēki o hiru-gohan ni ryōri shimasu. **7.** Haru watashi wa niwa o sōji shimasu. **8.** Tom-kun wa Nihon-go o benkyō shimasu ka.

Exercise 5: **1.** Do-yōbi no asa Makoto-kun wa tenisu o shimasu. **2.** Gogo Makoto-kun wa yakkū o shimasu. **3.** Ban Makoto-kun wa Eigo no benkyō o shimasu.

Exercise 6: Dore ni shimasu ka. – Kore ni shimasu.; Doko ni shimasu ka. – Koko ni shimasu.; Nan ni shimasu ka. – Kore ni shimasu.

Exercise 7: **1.** Could you take me to a hospital please? **2.** May I speak to Tom please? **3.** What fruit do we have? **4.** Which temple do we decide on? **5.** Who's house do we decide on? **6.** Tōkyō (no)* dōbutsuen onegai shimasu. (Tōkyō dōbutsuen is a personal pronoun meaning Tokyo Zoo while Tōkyō no dōbutsuen means Zoo in Tokyo.) **7.** Eigo no sensei onegai shimasu. **8.** Hanako-san ni purezento wa nan ni shimasu ka. **9.** Dare ni shimasu ka. **10.** Ryokō wa doko ni shimasu ka.

Exercise 8: **1.** Tom-kun to Hanako-san wa Edo e ikimasu. **2.** Tom-kun wa tonkatsu o tabemasu. **3.** Hanako-san wa yakisoba o tabemasu. **4.** Hanako-san wa miruku o nomimasu.

Exercise 1: **1.** abunai **2.** mezurashii **3.** tanoshii **4.** urusai **5.** isogashii **6.** akai **7.** aoi

Exercise 2: **2.** mezurashiku nai tori **3.** sabishiku nai (o)tera **4.** urusaku nai inu **5.** tanoshiku nai hi **6.** akaku nai ringo

Exercise 3: **2.** are **3.** asoko **4.** koko **5.** asoko **6.** sore

Exercise 4: **1.** blue eye **2.** large steak **3.** this dog **4.** not a frightful teacher (teacher who is not frightening) **5.** not a cold day **6.** (My) father goes to his work (company) in this black car. **7.** In summer, I and (my) younger brother learn easy Japanese. **8.** Do you read a difficult book at school? **9.** tsumetai mizu **10.** ōkii hito **11.** ano kodomo **12.** omoshiroku nai eiga **13.** Kore wa nagai kisha desu.

Exercise 5: **1.** Ano inu wa kowaku nai desu. **2.** Kono ringo wa oishiku nai desu. **3.** Mari-chan wa kawaiku nai desu. **4.** Kono hon wa omoshiroku nai desu. **5.** Kore wa muzukashiku nai desu.

Exercise 6: **1.** This summer is hot, isn't it? **2.** Betty's dog is dirty. **3.** This fruit is cheap! **4.** The sea water is cold, isn't it? **5.** A Japanese person is not rare. **6.** Kanada wa samui desu. **7.** Kore wa mezurashii desu. **8.** Igirisu wa omoshiroi desu ka. **9.** Gakkō wa tanoshii desu ka. **10.** Watashi no kasa wa kuroku nai desu.

Exercise 7: **2.** genki de nai inu, not an energetic (healthy) dog **3.** yūmei de nai (o)tera, not a famous temple

Exercise 8: **1.** a quiet temple **2.** a handsome man (person) **3.** Taro is an energetic (healthy) cat. **4.** This is my father's precious book. **5.** genki na neko **6.** kirei na me **7.** shinsetsu de nai hito **8.** Kore wa yūmei na e desu. **9.** Sono kodomo wa genki na kodomo desu.

Exercise 1: **1.** Watashi wa ringo ga suki desu. **2.** Watashi wa tenpura ga suki desu. **3.** Watashi wa ninjin ga kirai desu. **4.** Watashi wa miruku ga kirai desu. **5.** Watashi wa tenisu ga jōzu desu. **6.** Watashi wa Eigo ga jōzu desu. **7.** Watashi wa suiei ga heta desu. **8.** Watashi wa Nihon-go ga heta desu. **9.** Watashi wa sutēki ga hoshii desu. **10.** Watashi wa terebi ga hoshi desu.

Exercise 2: **1.** Onīsan wa suiei to tenisu to jūdō to taisō o shimasu. **2.** jōzu de wa arimasen. **3.** Iie suki de wa arimasen.

Exercise 3: **1.** the person whom somebody likes **2.** the book that somebody wants **3.** the teacher whom somebody does not dislike **4.** the meal that somebody does not want **5.** I like apples. (The apples are likeable fruit.) **6.** I read the book I dislike at school. (I read the dislikeable book at school.) **7.** That elephant wants your banana. **8.** kirai na sensei **9.** heta na Eigo **10.** jōzu de nai Nihon-go **11.** hoshiku nai nomimono **12.** Watashi wa Nihon-jin ga suki desu. **13.** Watashi wa ōkii sutēki ga ban-gohan ni hoshii desu. **14.** Anata wa dare ga suki desu ka.

Exercise 4: **1.** Watashi wa atama ga itai desu. **2.** Watashi wa ashi ga itai desu. **3.** Watashi wa ude ga itai desu. **4.** Watashi wa me ga itai desu. **5.** Watashi wa onaka ga itai desu.

Exercise 5: **1.** I have a pain in my stomach. (As for me, the stomach is painful.) **2.** Hanako has beautiful eyes. (As for Hanako, the eyes are beautiful.) **3.** Giraffes have long necks. (As for giraffes, the necks are long.) **4.** Japanese have low noses, don't they? (As for Japanese, the noses are low, aren't they?) **5.** Watashi wa ude ga kayui desu. **6.** Watashi wa ashi ga itai desu. **7.** Otōsan wa te ga ōkii desu. **8.** Zō wa hana ga nagai desu.

Exercise 1: **2.** nagaku **3.** usuku **4.** yasashiku **5.** tanoshiku

Exercise 2: **1.** totemo **2.** amari **3.** totemo **4.** amari

Exercise 3: **1.** Sugu **2.** Naze **3.** Yagate/Sorosoro **4.** Motto

Exercise 4: **1.** a very beautiful dress **2.** a very large person **3.** I will go there immediately **4.** Why do you like Hanako? **5.** Would you like to go to the party a bit early? **6.** totemo hayai kisha **7.** amari kawaiku nai neko **8.** Ōkii ie wa totemo takai desu ka. **9.** Otōto wa Eigo o totemo yukkuri hanashi-masu. **10.** Yagate/Sorosoro otōsan wa kimasu.

Exercise 5: **2.** Makoto-kun wa Hiroshi-kun yori hansamu desu. **3.** Ken-kun wa Chūgoku-go ga Nihon-go yori jōzu desu. **4.** Watashi wa yakyū ga tenisu yori suki desu. (Hiroshi-kun yori, Nihon-go yori and tenisu yori may be inserted before/after _ wa or before "adjective + desu.")

Exercise 6: **1.** Hikari wa Kodama yori hayai desu. **2.** Nozomi wa Hikari yori hayai desu. **3.** Kodama wa mottomo osoi desu. **4.** Nozomi wa mottomo hayai desu.

Exercise 7: **1.** Japanese houses are less spacious than Canadian houses. **2.** Americans have taller noses than Japanese have. **3.** I like geography much more than I like history. **4.** Sūgaku no sensei wa chiri no sensei yori shinsetsu desu. **5.** Kono inu wa (watashi no) otōto yori ōkii desu. **6.** Amerika no budō wa Nihon no budō yori motto yasui desu.

Exercise 1: **1.** shio, koshō, satō, shōyu, koppu **2.** neko, okāsan

Exercise 2: **1.** Okāsan wa sūpāmāketto de kaimono o shimasu. **2.** Hai imasu. **3.** Sūpāmāketto wa totemo benri desu. **4.** Iie arimasen. **5.** Kēki-ya ni oishii pan ga arimasu. **6.** Iie ikimasen.

Exercise 3: **1.** Over there, (there) is the department store. **2.** There is Makoto. **3.** (My) father and (my) mother are in the garden. **4.** There is neither salt nor pepper here. **5.** There is a cat in the kitchen. There is a cat in the garden also. **6.** What is here? **7.** Asoko ni otōsan no megane ga arimasu. **8.** Ano kudamono-ya ni totemo oishii ringo to orenji ga arimasu. **9.** Byōin ni (o)isha-san to kangofu-san ga imasu. **10.** Niwa ni Betty-san ga imasen. **11.** Doko ni ginkō ga arimasu ka. **12.** Asoko ni nani ga arimasu ka.

Exercise 4: **1.** Ashita Hanako-san wa (Eigo no) tesuto ga arimasu. **2.** Hai arimasu. **3.** Yoru onēsan wa deito ga arimasu. **4.** Iie arimasen. **5.** Otōsan wa kaigi ga arimasu. **6.** Okāsan wa pātī ga arimasu.

Exercise 5: **1.** We have an English test tomorrow morning. **2.** I have Hanako's birthday party tomorrow. **3.** Do you have (any) children? **4.** I don't have any time now. **5.** Watashi wa (o)kane ga arimasen. **6.** Otōsan wa kaigi ga Tōkyō de* arimasu. (*Note that meeting is an action/event taking place in Tokyo, and hence Tōkyō is followed by de and not ni.) **7.** Anata no heya ni terebi ga arimasu ka. **8.** Anata wa onīsan ga imasu ka.

Exercise 6: **1.** Iie yomimasen. **2.** Tom-kun to Makoto-kun wa sētā o Hanako-san ni kaimasu. **3.** Sētā wa akai desu. **4.** Sētā wa go-sen-en desu.

Exercise 1: **1.** no **2.** de **3.** no

Exercise 2: **1.** ie no naka **2.** ie no soto **3.** ie no chikaku **4.** ie no yoko **5.** ie no mae **6.** ie no ushiro **7.** tsukue no ue **8.** tsukue no shita

Exercise 3: **1.** ue **2.** yoko **3.** mae **4.** shita

Exercise 4: **1.** This dog drinks toilet water (water in a toilet). **2.** Your book is on the desk! **3.** (My) father and (my) mother are in the house. **4.** My younger brother reads cartoons in the bus. **5.** There is a hospital in front of the school. **6.** Nyūyōku no tatemono wa totemo takai desu. **7.** Tsukue no ue ni enpitsu ga arimasu. **8.** Umi no naka ni ōkii sakana ga imasu. **9.** Ano ōkii depāto no yoko ni yūbinkyoku ga arimasu. **10.** Daidokoro no tēburu no ue ni nani ga arimasu ka.

Exercise 5: **1.** Hidari-gawa ni jinja ga arimasu. **2.** Mae ni kawa ga arimasu. **3.** Hidari-gawa ni ginkō to yūbinkyoku to keisatsu-sho ga arimasu. Migi-gawa ni (o)tera to gakkō ga arimasu. Ushiro ni kawa ga arimasu. **4.** Migi-gawa ni byōin ga arimasu. **5.** Hidari-gawa ni gakkō ga arimasu.

Exercise 6: **1.** Kōsaten o migi e magarimasu. **2.** Kōsaten o hidari e magari-masu. **3.** Kōsaten o massugu ikimasu. **4.** Tsukiatari o migi e magarimasu **5.** Tsukiatari o hidari e magarimasu

Exercise 7: **1.** I will go straight along this road. **2.** The bus will turn right at the traffic light. **3.** Turn left at that T-junction. **4.** The number three bus will go to Higashi Park. **5.** I will stop the car at the opposite side of the temple. **6.** Ano shingō o massugu ikimasu. **7.** Tsukiatari o migi e magari-masu. **8.** Kono basu wa Atago-yama no hō e ikimasu. **9.** Eki no hantai-gawa ni pan-ya ga arimasu. **10.** Ano hoteru no mae o migi e magarimasu.

Exercise 1: **2.** ga, The bus will come soon. **3.** ga, The movie will start im-mediately. **4.** wa, This summer, I will start a study of English. **5.** ga, The train will move!

Exercise 2: **1.** Otōsan wa roku-ji han ni okimasu. **2.** Iie ikimasen. **3.** Otōsan wa kuruma no kaisha de hatarakimasu. **4.** Yoru shichi-ji ni otōsan wa uchi e kaerimasu.

Exercise 3: **1.** Nichi-yōbi wa kumori matawa ame desu. **2.** Getsu-yōbi wa hare desu. **3.** Ka-yōbi wa yuki ga furimasu.   or   Ka-yōbi wa yuki desu. **4.** Sui-yōbi wa kumori desu. **5.** Moku-yōbi wa ame ga furimasu.   or   Moku-yōbi wa ame desu. **6.** Kin-yōbi wa kumori matawa hare desu. **7.** Do-yōbi wa hare matawa kumori desu.

Exercise 4: **1.** It will snow tomorrow. **2.** In June, (my) older brother's house will be completed. (house will be made) **3.** My younger brother swims in the pool with (his) friend. **4.** A car stops in front of the house. **5.** (My) father works at a car factory. **6.** A baby does not cry in its mother's arms. **7.** What time does the Japanese movie starts? **8.** Yagate/Sorosoro ame ga yamimasu. **9.** Itsu ano yama no yuki ga tokemasu ka. **10.** Okāsan no koe ga tonari no ie kara kikoemasu. **11.** Natsu watashi wa umi de oyogimasu.

12. Yama ga miemasu. **13.** Haru watashi wa ojisan ni Kanada de aimasu. **14.** San-gatsu ni onīsan wa Amerika e ugokimasu.

Exercise 5: **1.** okāsan **2.** otōsan **3.** Tom-kun **4.** Tom-kun

Exercise 6: **1.** Do you understand this picture (painting)? **2.** I understand Japanese a little. **3.** What (kind of) sports can you do? **4.** (My) younger brother cannot drive a car. **5.** He (That person) cannot speak (do) Japanese at all! **6.** Watashi wa Hanako-san ga zenzen wakarimasen. **7.** (Watashi no) otōto wa jūdō ga dekimasen. **8.** Watashi wa benkyō ga ie de dekimasen. **9.** Okāsan wa Eigo ga zenzen dekimasen. **10.** Anata wa Hanako-san no Eigo ga wakarimasu ka.

Exercise 1: **2.** yasashikatta desu yo, Yesterday's test was easy! **3.** suki deshita, I liked Hanako last year. **4.** sui-yōbi de wa arimasen deshita yo, Yesterday wasn't a Wednesday! **5.** samuku nakatta desu ne, Yesterday wasn't cold, was it?

Exercise 2: **1.** Tom-kun wa Amerika e ikimashita. **2.** Tom-kun wa obasan to ojisan no ie ni tomarimashita. **3.** Hai shimashita. **4.** Tom-kun wa kari-horunia ga ichiban suki deshita. **5.** Tom-kun wa terebi o mimashita. **6.** Tom-kun wa Eigo o hanashimashita. **7.** Hai suzushikatta desu. **8.** Tom-kun no natsu-yasumi wa tanoshii natsu-yasumi deshita.

Exercise 3: **1.** He (That person) was Makoto's older brother. **2.** Yesterday, I heard French songs (French songs were heard) at the youth hostel. **3.** Last summer, there was a big tree here. **4.** Last month, we did shopping in America. **5.** Yesterday, I made a chair with (my) father. **6.** What did you eat for lunch yesterday? **7.** Are wa (o)tera deshita. **8.** Kyonen watashi wa Amerika e hikōki de ikimashita. **9.** Kinō tsukue no ue ni shinbun ga arimashita. **10.** Nagai ryokō ga owarimashita. **11.** Kinō no ban watashi wa ban-gohan o tabemasen deshita. **12.** Kinō watashi wa tenisu o Makoto-kun to shimasen deshita.

Exercise 1: **1.** ashita, rainen, rai-shū, asatte, korekara, rai-getsu **2.** sen-shū, sen-getsu, ototoi, kinō, kyonen

Exercise 2: **1.** The day after tomorrow will be a Monday. **2.** Tomorrow, (my) father and (my) mother will return from Britain. **3.** Next week, (my) older brother's house will be completed (made). **4.** The day after tomorrow, I will eat dinner at Betty's house. **5.** Tomorrow's movie will not be interesting! **6.** Tomorrow, I will wait for you at the station, will I? **7.** Next week, I will return this book to you. **8.** Tomorrow, I will not play tennis. **9.** The school will start next Wednesday (Wednesday of next week). **10.** Would you like to go shopping next week? **11.** Ashita wa nichi-yōbi desu. **12.** Itsuka watashi wa Furansu-go o naraimasu (benkyō shimasu). **13.** Ashita otōto to watashi wa (o)tera e ikimasu. **14.** Ashita anata wa nani o shimasu ka. **15.** Ashita no asa watashi wa yama no e o kakimasu. **16.** Rainen anata no ojīsan wa Nihon e kimasu ka. **17.** Ashita watashi wa terebi o mimasen. **18.** Rai-nen watashi wa aoi takai kōto o kaimasu. **19.** Rai-getsu akachan ga obasan ni umaremasu. **20.** Ashita watashi wa kono doresu o kimasu.

Exercise 3: **1.** Tom – a medical doctor, Mari – a nurse, Makoto – a judo instructor, Hanako – a school teacher, Ken – a white-collar worker

Exercise 4:

Adjective	Meaning	"Adjective + desu"	Meaning	Future Tense
nagai	long	nagai desu	to be long	nagaku narimasu
hoshii	desirous	hoshii desu	to be desirable	hoshiku narimasu
muzukashii	difficult	muzukashii desu	to be difficult	muzukashiku narimasu
benri na	convenient	benri desu	to be convenient	benri ni narmasu
rippa na	splendid	rippa desu	to be splendid	rippa ni narimasu

Exercise 5: **1.** Kyō wa samui desu. **2.** Gogo wa atatakaku narimasu. **3.** Hachi-gatsu wa totemo atsuku narimasu. **4.** Ku-gatsu wa hachi-gatsu yori suzushii desu.

Exercise 6: **1.** Next month, (my) aunt Akiko will become a mother. **2.** Will the study of Japanese language be difficult? **3.** Someday, he (that person) will be famous! **4.** After a party, the kitchen will be dirty. **5.** You will like Japanese history! **6.** Itsuka anata wa tenisu ga jōzu ni narimasu. **7.** Itsuka anata wa (o)isha-san ni narimasu ka. **8.** Rainen sukāto wa mijikaku narimasu yo. **9.** Kono ki wa ōkiku narimasen. **10.** Anata wa Nihon no tabemono ga suki ni narimasu.

Exercise 1: **2.** Let's buy this sweater. **3.** Let's wait for Hanako until three o'clock here. **4.** Let's show this to (our) teacher tomorrow. **5.** Let's trurn ight at that traffic light. **6.** Let's walk to the mountain. **7.** Let's move (our) ather's desk.

Exercise 2: **1.** Let's meet in front of the department store at eight o'clock omorrow. **2.** Let's give this apple to (our) grandpa. **3.** Let's invite a friend or lunch tomorrow. **4.** Let's buy this. **5.** Let's swim in the sea in summer. **.** Let's study (from) now. **7.** Kyō no yoru terebi o mimashō. **8.** Rainen Nihon-go o naraimashō (benkyō shimashō). **9.** Atatakai sētāo kaimashō.

10. Ban-gohan o tabemashō. **11.** Ashita no asa depāto e basu de ikimashō. **12.** Asobimashō.

Exercise 3: **2.** Drink plenty of water! **3.** Speak Japanese at home! **4.** Return that to Mari! **5.** Go to school! **6.** Put on a much longer skirt!

Exercise 4: **1.** Tom-kun wa atama ga itai desu. **2.** Hai ikimashita. **3.** Hai agemashita. **4.** Kyō to ashita Tom-kun wa kusuri o nomimasu.

Exercise 5: **1.** Amy, write your letter in (your) room! **2.** Robert, give milk to the cat! **3.** Kimi and Betty, go to the school by bus tomorrow! **4.** Tom, play outside! **5.** Betty, study French! **6.** Betty wa heya no sōji o shinasai (heya o sōji shinasai). **7.** Makoto wa gakkō e ikinasai. **8.** Robert wa tomato o tabenasai. **9.** Kimi wa koko e kinasai. **10.** Gohan no mae ni Tom wa te o arainasai.

Lesson 25

Exercise 1: **1.** dareka **2.** dokoka **3.** itsuka **4.** dare demo **5.** doko demo **6.** itsu demo **7.** dare mo **8.** doko mo **9.** itsu mo

Exercise 2: **1.** Watashi wa dono hon ka yomimasu; Watashi wa dono hon demo yomimasu; Watashi wa dono hon mo yomimasen. **2.** Watashi wa nanika kaimasu; Watashi wa nan demo kaimasu; Watashi wa nani mo kaimasen. **3.** Watashi wa kore o dareka ni agemasu; Watashi wa kore o dare ni demo agemasu; Watashi wa kore o dare ni mo agemasen.

Exercise 3: **1.** I don't want anything. **2.** I will not buy any of them. **3.** Would you like to drink something? **4.** I will read something. **5.** Would someone like to watch this video? **6.** Nobody went to the mountain. **7.** I will play tennis anytime! **8.** Kono inu wa nan demo tabemasu. **9.** Watashi wa dono kudamono mo kaimasen. **10.** Dokoka e ikimasen ka. **11.** Watashi wa nani mo mimasen deshita. **12.** Watashi wa dono doresu mo kaimasen. **13.** Makoto-kun wa itsu mo pātī ni kimasen. **14.** Itsuka yama e ikimasen ka.

Lesson 26

Exercise 1:

V.masu	Meaning	"Want to" Form	"Don't Want to" Form
naraimasu	learn	naraitai desu	naraitaku nai desu
okurimasu	send	okuritai desu	okuritaku nai desu
shimasu	do	shitai desu	shitaku nai desu
aimasu	meet	aitai desu	aitaku nai desu
kimasu	come	kitai desu	kitaku nai desu

Exercise 2: 1. I want to eat a watermelon. 2. I want to go to the Christmas party. 3. I want to get up early in the morning. 4. I want to stay (be) here. 5. I want to go somewhere.

Exercise 3: 1. Which magazine do you want to read? 2. I want to cry now. 3. (My) older brother wants to swim in the river. 4. I don't want to eat (my) dinner today. 5. I don't want to study. 6. Kyō no yoru watashi wa bideo ga mitai desu. 7. Watashi wa sutēki ga ban-gohan ni tabetai desu. 8. Watashi wa arukitai desu. 9. Ano neko wa heya kara detai desu. 10. Okāsan wa Itaria no handobaggu ga kaitai desu.

Exercise 4: 1. Watashi wa suika ga tabetakatta desu. 2. Watashi wa Kurisumasu pātī ni ikitakatta desu. 3. Watashi wa asa hayaku okitakatta desu. 4. Watashi wa koko ni itakatta desu. 5. Watashi wa dokoka e ikitakatta desu.

Exercise 5: 1. I wanted to draw a picture of the mountain. 2. Last year, (my) grandfather wanted to return to America. 3. During (In) the summer holiday, (my) older sister wanted to work. 4. I wanted to do shopping in town. 5. Kyonen watashi wa Igirisu e ikitakatta desu. 6. Okāsan wa totemo takai doresu ga kaitakatta desu. 7. Watashi wa kuruma ga unten shitakatta desu. 8. Watashi wa kōhī ga nomitakatta desu.

Exercise 6: 1. Watashi wa suika ga tabetaku nakatta desu. 2. Watashi wa Kurisumasu pātī ni ikitaku nakatta desu. 3. Watashi wa asa hayaku okitaku nakatta desu. 4. Watashi wa koko ni itaku nakatta desu. 5. Watashi wa doko e mo ikitaku nakatta desu.

Exercise 7: 1. Last year, I did not want to come to Japan. 2. I did not want to get off the train. 3. (My) younger brother did not want to learn French. 4. (My) father did not want to buy this car. 5. Watashi wa Doitsu e ikitaku nakatta desu. 6. Watashi wa Robert-kun o pātī ni manekitaku nakatta desu. 7. Watashi wa anata ni aitaku nakatta desu. 8. Kinō imōto wa sūgaku ga/o benkyō shitaku nakatta desu (sūgaku no benkyō ga/o shitaku nakatta desu).

Lesson 27

Exercise 1: 1. ikitai toki 2. ikitaku nai toki 3. ikitakatta toki 4. ikitaku nakatta toki 5. aitai hito 6. aitaku nai hito 7. aitakatta hito 8. aitaku nakatta hito

Exercise 2: 1. c 2. f 3. d 4. h 5. e 6. a 7. g 8. b

Exercise 3: 1. I don't have anything (a thing) I want to do. 2. This is the place I wanted to visit (come). 3. The person I wanted to see (meet) has gone to America. 4. This is the fruit I wanted to eat. 5. The bus that I wanted to get on has gone. 6. Today, I will eat the fruit that I did not want to eat yesterday. 7. Kono mise ni kaitai mono ga arimasen. 8. Watashi wa shitaku nai koto o shimasen. 9. Kinō watashi wa mitakatta eiga o mi-nashita. 10. Kore wa yomitakatta hon desu. 11. Onīsan wa ikitaku nakatta pātī ni ikimashita. 12. Korekara kinō yomitaku nakatta hon o yomimasu.

Exercise 4:

Meaning	Present	Negative Present	Past	Negative Past
big	ōkii	ōkiku nai	ōkikatta	ōkiku nakatta
red	akai	akaku nai	akakatta	akaku nakatta
busy	isogashii	isogashiku nai	isogashikatta	isogashiku nakatta
healthy	genki na	genki de nai	genki datta	genki de nakatta
convenient	benri na	benri nai	benri datta	benri de nakatta
likeable	suki na	suki de (wa) nai	suki datta	suki de (wa) nakatta

Exercise 5: 1. (My) younger brother does not like hot (spicy) Indian curry. 2. Yesterday, we watched a boring (not interesting) movie at (our) school. 3. The book store didn't have the book I wanted. 4. I wrote things about (my) unhappy times. (I wrote things about the time that was not enjoyable.) 5. I want to be a splendid doctor. 6. Inconvenient (Not convenient) apartments are cheap. 7. The kind person was Hanako's older sister. 8. Hanako became good at tennis, which she was not good at a long time ago. 9. Nagai ryokō ga owarimashita. 10. Abunaku nai tokoro e ikimashō. 11. Ano inu (Are) wa urusakatta inu de wa arimasen. 12. Watashi wa amari takaku nai doresu o kaimashita. 13. Kinō watashi wa baka na koto o shimashita. 14. Amari benri de nai tokoro ni watashi-tachi wa sumimashita. 15. Suki data hito wa kekkon shimashita.

Exercise 1: 1. Konnichiwa, Good afternoon. 2. Tadaima, I am back. 3. Sumimasen, Excuse me. 4. mikan, tangerine orange 5. ringo, apple 6. yasai, vegetable 7. kudamono, fruit 8. sensei, teacher 9. inu, dog
Exercise 2: 1. ともだち 2. あなた 3. はなこさん 4. ごめんなさい 5. うさぎ 6. にほんご 7. がいこく 8. こども 9. ねこ 10. ねずみ
Exercise 3: 2. o 3. a 4. o 5. o 6. o 7. o 8. o 9. u 10. o
Exercise 4: 1. おとうさん 2. おじいさん 3. おばあさん 4. いもうと 5. おとうと 6. どうぶつえん 7. にっぽん 8. きっさてん 9. ざっし 10. がっこう
Exercise 5: 1. Koko wa eki desu, This is a (railway) station. 2. Kore wa watashi no inu desu, This is my dog. 3. Anata wa sushi o tabemasu ka, Do you eat sushi? 4. Ashita watashi-tachi wa yama e ikimasu, Tomorrow, we will go to the mountain. 5. Korekara anata wa nani o shimasu ka, What do you

do from now? **6.** Asoko ni kudamono-ya ga arimasu, Over there is the fruit shop. **7.** Watashi wa Hanako desu, I am Hanako.

Exercise 1: **1.** スミス **2.** ロンドン **3.** アメリカ **4.** イギリス **5.** パリ **6.** フランス **7.** ペン **9.** クラス **10.** ワイン **11.** ワシントン

Exercise 2: 1. orenji, orange **2.** toire, toilet **3.** rajio, radio **4.** banana, banana **5.** pen, pen **6.** purezento, present

Exercise 3: **1.** ノート **2.** ジュース **3.** ニューヨーク **4.** テーブル **5.** スカート **6.** アイスクリーム **7.** タクシー **8.** コップ **9.** コーヒー **10.** ーター

Exercise 4: 1. Watashi no okāsan wa Amerika-jin desu, My mother is American. **2.** Otōsan wa rajio o niwa de kikimasu, (My) father listens to the radio in the garden. **3.** Makoto-kun wa terebi o mimasen, Makoto does not watch TV. **4.** Smith-san wa kōhī o nomimasu, Mr. Smith drinks coffee. **5.** Watashi-tachi wa sutēki o tabemashita, We ate steak. **6.** Toire wa doko desu ka, Where is a toilet?

Exercise 1: 1. d **2.** a **3.** g **4.** b **5.** e **6.** h **7.** f **8.** c

Vocabulary

A

abunai dangerous

achira that person *(a person away from the speaker and the listener"*

agemasu give (to somebody)

ahiru duck

aidea idea

aimasu meet

aisatsu greeting

aisukurīmu ice cream

akachan baby

akai red

aki autumn

amai sweet (taste)

amari (not) very *(with negative adjectives and adverbs describing negative verbs)*; (not) a lot, (not) much *(with negative verbs)*

ame candy

ame rain

Amerika America

amimono knitting

anata you

ano that (over there)

aoi blue

apāto apartment

araimasu wash

are that *(a thing/person away from the speaker and the listener)*

arigatō thank you

arimasu to be located/to exist *(to describe a non-living subject)*

arukimasu walk

asa morning

asa-gohan breakfast

asatte the day after tomorrow

ashi leg

ashita tomorrow

asobimasu play, amuse, enjoy

asoko that (place over there) *(a place away from both the speaker and the listener)*

atama head

atatakai warm

ato (time) after

atsui hot (of touch)

atsui hot (temperature)

atsui thick (of flat things)

atsumemasu collect

B

baka na foolish, stupid

-ban *put after numbers to tell the order*

ban evening

banana banana

ban-gohan dinner

banira vanilla

basu bus

bāsudē birthday

basu-sutoppu bus stop

benkyō study

benri na convenient

bentō meal in a box

bideo video

boku I, me *(for boys)*

bōshi hat

budō grape

burausu blouse

burūsu blues

buta pig

buta-niku pork

byōin hospital

C

cha Japanese green tea
chairoi brown
-chan *added after the names of small children, especially girls*
chawan bowl (rice)
chekkuauto check out
chiisai small, quiet *(sound, voice)*
chikaku nearby
chiri geography
chizu map
chokorēto chocolate
chūgakkō secondary school
Chūgoku China

D

daidokoro kitchen
daigaku university, college
daikon large white radish
dakara so, therefore
dakkusufundo dachshund
dame na not good
dare who
dare mo (not) anyone
dareka somebody
de in/with/by
deito date
dekimasu be made, be produced, be possible
demasu go out
densha electric train
depāto department store
desu is, am, are
dewa mata see you (later)

dō how, in what way
dōbutsu animal
dōbutsuen zoo
Doitsu Germany
doko where, which place
doko mo (not) anywhere
dokoka somewhere
dono which
dore which one
dore mo (not) any of them
doreka something
doresu dress
dōro road, way, highway
do-yōbi Saturday
dōzo please

E

e picture, painting
e to *(motion towards a "place")*
eiga movie
Eigo English language
eki (railway) station
-en _yen
enpitsu pencil
erabimasu choose

F

fuben na inconvenient
fuku cloth
funabin surface mail
fune ship, boat
Furansu France
furimasu fall *(rain, snow)*
furo bath
furoba bathroom
futoi thick *(of cylindrical things)*, fat

futsuka 2nd *(day of the month)*
fuyu winter

G

gaijin foreigner
gaikoku abroad
gakkō school
gakusei student *(in a school)*
-gatsu *put after a number to tell the month*
-gawa -side
genki na healthy, hearty
getsu-yōbi Monday
ginkō bank
-go *added to the name of a country for its language*
go five
Gochisōsama. Thank you for the food. *(after eating)*
go-gatsu May
gogo p.m. *(also **gozen**)*
gohan meal, boiled rice
go-kai fifth floor
gōkei total
gomennasai sorry
goshujin somebody else's husband
gyū-niku beef

H

hachi eight
hachi-gatsu August
hai yes
hairimasu come in, enter, join, get in
ha-isha dentist
hajimarimasu begin

Hajimemashite. How do you do?
hajimemasu begin
hajimete for the first time
hakarimasu measure, weigh
hakimasu put on *(footwear, trousers)*
hakusai Chinese cabbage
han half past *(time)*
hana flower
hana nose
hanashi talk, conversation
hanashimasu speak
hana-ya flower shop
hanbāgā hamburger
handobaggu handbag
hansamu na handsome
hantai opposite
hare fine weather
haru spring
hashi chopsticks
hatarakimasu work
hayai quick, rapid, early
hayaku quickly, rapidly, early
hebi snake
hen na strange, suspicious
heta na bad *(at a particular skill)*
heya room
hi day
hidari left
-hiki *put after a number to count animals such as dogs, tigers, rabbits, fishes and insects*
hikōjō airport
hikōki airplane
hikui low, short *(height)*
hima free, time to spare

hiroi spacious
hiru afternoon
hiru-gohan lunch
hito person
hō direction
hokenshō health insurance card
hōkō direction
hōku fork
hon book
hone bone
hon-ya bookstore
hoshii desirous
hosoi thin *(cylindrical things)*
hoteru hotel
hyaku 100
hyaku-man 1,000,000

I ―――――――――――――

ichi one
ichi-ban most, best, number one
ichi-gatsu January
ichigo strawberry
ie house, home
Igirisu Britain
ii good
iie no
ike pond
ikimasu go
ik-kai first floor
ikura how much
ima at this moment
ima family room
imasu to be located/to exist *(to describe a living subject)*
imōto younger sister
inu dog

ippai full, plenty
ip-pun one minute
Irasshaimase. Hello and welcome. Come in.
iro color
isha physician, medical doctor
isogashii busy
isu chair
Itadakimasu. Thank you for the gift. *(when receiving)*, Thank you for the food. *(before eating)*
itai painful
Itaria Italy
itsu when
itsu mo (not) anytime
itsuka 5th *(day of the month)*
itsuka someday

J ―――――――――――――

jagaimo potato
jazu jazz
jidō-kippu-uriba automatic ticket dispensing area
jidōsha automobile
jikan (spare) time
jikanhyō timetable
-jin *added to the name of a country to describe its inhabitants*
jinja shrine
jitensha bicycle
jōzu na good *(at a particular skill)*
jū ten
jūdō judo
jū-gatsu October
jugyō lecture
jūichi-gatsu November
juku cram school

jū-man 100,000
jūni-gatsu December
jūsu juice

K

ka or, *put at the end of a phrase to indicate "?"*
kaban briefcase
kaburimasu put on *(hat)*
kaeri return
kaerimasu to return
kaeshimasu return *(things borrowed)*
kagaku science
kagi key
kaigi meeting
kaimasu buy
kaimono shopping
kaisha company
kaishain white-collar worker
kakimasu write, draw
kami hair
Kanada Canada
kanai my wife
kane money
kangofu nurse
kao face
kara from
karada body
karai spicy
karate karate
karēraisu Indian curry
karimasu borrow
karui light *(weight)*
kasa umbrella
kashimasu lend
kata shoulder

kawa river
kawaii cute
ka-yōbi Tuesday
kayui itchy
kaze a cold
kazoku family
kēki cake
kēki-ya cake shop
kekkon marriage
kesa this morning
keshō make-up
kibun feeling
kiiroi yellow
kikimasu listen to, hear, ask for
kikoemasu be heard
kimarimasu be decided
kimasu come
kimasu put on *(dress)*
kimono kimono
kinō yesterday
kin-yōbi Friday
kirai na detestable, dislikeable
kirei na beautiful, clean
kirin giraffe
kisha train
kissaten coffee shop
kitanai dirty
kitte stamp
kōcha Indian tea
kochira this person *(to describe a person near the speaker)*
kodomo child
koe voice, cry
kōen park
kōgyō-daigaku technical college
kōhī coffee
kōjō factory

koko this place *(to describe a place near the speaker)*
kōkō high school
kokonoka 9th *(day of the month)*
kōkūbin air mail
kokugo the national language
konban this evening
konbanwa good evening
kon-getsu this month
konnichiwa good afternoon, hello
kono this
kon-shū this week
koppu cup
kore this *(to describe a thing/person near the speaker)*
korekara from now on
kōsaten intersection
koshō pepper
koto thing *(abstract)*
kōto coat
kotoshi this year
kowai frightful, frightening
kowaremasu break
kowashimasu break (something)
ku nine
kuchi mouth
kudamono fruit
kudamono-ya fruit shop
ku-gatsu September
kuma bear
kumo cloud
kumori cloudy weather
-kun *added after the names of boys*
kuni country
kurashikku myūjikku classical music
kurasu (lecture) class
kuremasu give (to me)

Kurisumasu Christmas
kuroi black
kuruma car
kurushii difficult
kusuri medicine
kutsu shoe
kutsushita sock, stocking
kyō today
kyonen last year
kyū nine
kyūri cucumber

M

machi town
machimasu wait for
mada yet *(used with negative verbs)*
made until, to
mae before/to *(time)*
mae front part, position in front
magarimasu turn
-mai *put after a number to count thin flat objects such as stamps, papers, tickets, plates, blankets, etc.*
mai-asa every morning
mai-ban every evening
mai-nen every year
mai-nichi every day
mai-shū every week
māmā so and so
man 10,000
manekimasu invite
manga comics, cartoon
manshon high-grade apartment
massugu straight through
mata again
matawa or
mazui unsavory taste

me eye

megane eyeglasses

mezurashii unusual, rare

michi road, path, way

midori-no-madoguchi train reservation office

miemasu be visible

migi right

mijikai short *(length)*

mikan tangerine

mikisā blender

mikka 3rd *(day of the month)*

mimai a visit *(to inquire about someom's health)*

mimasu see, watch

mimi ear

minikui ugly

minna everyone

miokurimasu see someone off

miruku milk

mise shops

misemasu show

mizu water

mizūmi lake

mo also/too

mō already

moku-yōbi Thursday

momo peach

mono thing *(article)*

moshi-moshi hello *(used only on the telephone)*

motto more

mottomo most, best

muika 6th *(day of the month)*

mukashi long time ago

muzukashii difficult

N

nagai long

naifu knife

naka middle, inside

nakimasu cry

nakushimasu lose

namae name

nan what

nana seven

nani what

nani mo (not) anything

nanika something

nanoka 7th *(day of the month)*

naraimasu learn

narimasu become

nashi pear

natsu summer

naze why

ne ... isn't it?, ... don't you?

negai appeal, wish

neko cat

nemasu sleep

-nen *put after a number to tell the year*

netsu body temperature, fever

nezumi mouse, rat

ni two

ni at/in/on

ni *used to indicate motion towards an event and direction of attention or interest*

-nichi *put after some numbers to tell the day of the month*

nichi-yōbi Sunday

nigai bitter (taste)

ni-gatsu February

Nihon Japan
niji rainbow
niku meat
niku-ya butcher's shop
-nin *put after a number to count people*
ninjin carrot
Nippon Japan
niwa garden
nomimasu drink, take *(medicine)*
nomimono drinks
norimasu ride (on)
nōto notebook
nyūin admission into a hospital

O

obasan aunt
obāsan grandmother
ohayōgozaimasu good morning
oishii delicious, tasty
ojisan uncle
ojīsan grandfather
okaerinasai welcome back
okāsan mother
okashi confectionery, sweets, candy
okashi-ya confectionery shop
ōkii big
ōkii loud *(sound, voice)*
ōkiku big
okimasu wake up
okuremasu be late
okurimasu send
okusan somebody else's wife
Ōmisoka New Year's Eve
omocha-ya toy shop
omoi heavy
omoshiroi interesting, amusing

omoshiroku interestingly
onaka stomach, abdomen, belly
onēsan older sister
ongaku music
onīsan older brother
orenji orange
orimasu break *(bone, stick)*
orimasu get off
osoi late, slow
osoku late
otearai washroom *(polite)*
ōtobai motorcycle
otona adult
otōsan father
otōto younger brother
ototoi the day before yesterday
oyasuminasai good night
oyogimasu swim
ōzei many people

P

painappuru pineapple
pan bread
pan-ya bread shop
Pari Paris
pātī party
pen pen
pittari na perfectly fit
poppu songu popular song
purattohōmu platform
purezento present
pūru pool

R

rai- next
rai-getsu next month

rainen next year
raion lion
rai-shū next week
rajio radio
ranchi lunch
reizōko refrigerator
rekishi history
resutoran restaurant
rikō na clever
ringo apple
rippa na splendid
risu squirrel
roku six
roku-gatsu June
romanchikku na romantic
Rondon London
ryokan Japanese inn
ryokō travel
ryōri cooking
ryūkōka popular song

S _____

sabishii lonely
saifu wallet, purse
sakana fish
sakana-ya fish shop
sakaya liquor store
sake Japanese rice wine
sakki a little while ago
sakuranbo cherry
samui cold *(temperature)*
-san Mr., Mrs., Ms *(after a name)*
san three
sandoicchi sandwich
san-gatsu March
sangurasu sunglasses

sansū arithmetic
sara plate
sarada salad
saru monkey
satō sugar
sayōnara good-bye
se height, stature
seito student *(general)*
semai limited *(space)*
sen- last
sen 1,000
sen (train) line
sen-getsu last month
senpūki electric fan
-sensei *added after the names of teachers and medical doctors*
sensei teacher
sen-shū last week
sentaku laundry
sētā sweater
shi four
shichi seven
shichi-gatsu July
shi-gatsu April
shigoto work
shimasu do
shinbun newspaper
shingō traffic light
shinimasu die
shinsetsu na kind
shio salt
shio-karai salty
shiroi white
shita lower part, space underneath
shiteiseki reserved seats
shizuka na quiet, peaceful

shōgakkō primary school

Shōgatsu New Year's Day

shōyu soy sauce

shujin my husband

shukudai homework

shumi hobby

shuto capitals

sō so, in that way

sochira that person *(indicates a person near the listener)*

sōji cleaning

soko that place *(indicates a place near the listener)*

sono that

sora sky

sore that thing *(indicates a thing/person near the listener)*

sorekara after that, and then

soto outside

sūgaku mathematics

sugi after/past *(time)*

sugu immediately

suiei swimming

suika watermelon

sui-yōbi Wednesday

sukāto skirt

sukī ski, skiing

suki na likable

sukimasu be empty, not crowded

sukoshi a little

sukūtā scooter

sumimasen excuse me, pardon me

sumimasu live at, take up residence

sumō sumo wrestling

sūpāmāketto supermarket

supōtsu sport

supūn spoon

sutēki steak

suteki na lovely

sutereo stereo

sūtsu suit

suzushii cool *(temperature)*

T

tabemasu eat

tabemono food

-tachi *added to make a person into a plural form*

Tadaima. I am back (now).

taihen very *(with adjectives and adverbs)*; a lot, much *(with verbs)*

taiin discharge from a hospital

taionkei clinical thermometer

taisetsu na precious

taisō gymnastics

takai expensive, high, tall

takaku expensively, highly

takusan much, many, a lot, plenty

takushī taxi

tamago egg

tamanegi onion

tanoshii enjoyable

tanoshiku enjoyably

tanuki badger

tatemono building

te hand

tēburu table

tegami letter

ten mark, score

tenisu tennis

tenki weather

tera temple

terebi television

tesuto test

tetsudai help

-tō *put after a number to count animals such as whales, cows and horses*

to and, together, along with

toire washroom

tōka 10th *(day of the month)*

tokei watch

tokemasu melt

toki time, moment

tokidoki sometimes

tokkyū super express (train)

tokoro place

Tōkyō Tokyo

tomarimasu stay (overnight), stop

tomato tomato

tomemasu stop (something)

tomodachi friend

tonari next door, position next to

tonkatsu pork cutlet

tora tiger

torakku truck

tori bird

torimasu score

torimasu take

tori-niku chicken meat

tōsutā toaster

totemo very *(with adjectives and adverbs)*; a lot, much *(with verbs)*

tsuitachi 1st *(day of the month)*

tsukaremasu be tired

tsukiatari T-intersection

tsukimasu arrive

tsukimasu be accompanied, be included

tsukue desk

tsukurimasu make

tsumaranai boring

tsumetai cold *(to the touch)*

tsuri change

U

uchi house, home

ude arm

ue upper part, space above

uētā waiter

uētoresu waitress

ugokashimasu move (something)

ugokimasu move

uma horse

umaremasu to be born

umi sea

undō-gutsu sport shoes

unten driving

urimasu sell

urusai noisy

usagi rabbit

ushi cow

ushiro back part, position behind

usui thin (of flat things)

uta song

W

-wa *put after a number to count animals such as rabbits, and birds such as ducks and chickens*

wain wine

wakarimasu to be understandable

wanpīsu one-piece dress

warui bad
Washinton Washington
wasuremasu forget
watashi I, me *(except young boys)*

Y

-ya -shop
yagate soon, presently, before long
yakusoku promise
yakyū baseball
yama mountain
yamemasu resign from, cease, stop
yamimasu stop *(rain, snow)*
yaoya vegetable shop
yasai vegetables
yasashii easy
yasashii gentle
yasui cheap
yasuku cheaply
yasumi holiday
yasumimasu be absent from, rest from, take time off from
yo *put at the end of a phrase to indicate "!"*
-yōbi *denotes the day of the week*
yōchien kindergarten
yoi good
yōka 8th *(day of the month)*
yokka 4th *(day of the month)*
yoko side part, position beside
yoku well, fully, often, a lot
yomimasu read
yon four
yori (more) than __
yoru night
yubi finger

yūbinkyoku post office
yuki snow
yukkuri slowly
yūmei na famous
yūsuhosuteru youth hostel

Z

zasshi magazine
zenbu all, everything, completely
zenzen not at all, entirely *(used with negative verbs)*
zero zero
zō elephant
zubon trousers

WEL

Please return / renew by date shown.
You can renew it at:
norlink.norfolk.gov.uk
or by telephone: 0344 800 8006
Please have your library card & PIN ready

25. 10. 16.
11. 11. 16.
29. 11. 16.

NORFOLK LIBRARY
AND INFORMATION SERVICE

NORFOLK ITEM

30129 077 632 629

Also by Niven Govinden:

We Are the New Romantics
Graffiti My Soul
Black Bread White Beer